Carol Deacon's
SPORTY CAKES

Carol Deacon's SPORTY CAKES

MEREHURST

CONTENTS

WATER SPORTS 8

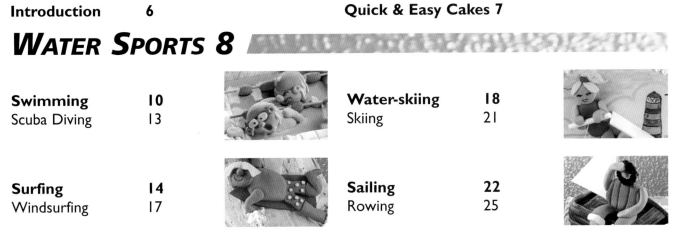

TEAM SPORTS 26

BALL SPORTS 46

DEDICATION
For Ismay, Eric, Cassie and Ebony Goodliff
for their participation in the noble sport of dog-sitting whilst this book was being written!

TRACK AND FIELD 60

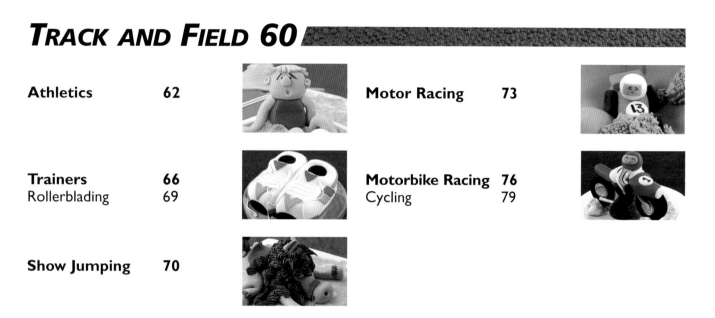

SOLO SPORTS 80

INTRODUCTION

When I first sat down to put together a book of sports cakes, I started with a list and a vague thought that it should probably feature about twenty or so designs. This soon became impossible as the list of sports kept getting longer and longer. I have done my best to include as many as possible. Hopefully, there will be something in here for everyone. If I have missed out your sport – many apologies – maybe it will be included in the next book.

Most of the designs involve working with sugarpaste (rolled fondant). If you are not exactly sure what that is, or you cannot get hold of it, have a look in the Icing Recipes and Techniques on pages 106 and 108 for more information. You can also use marzipan instead of sugarpaste.

I realize that there often are not enough hours in the day to make an all-singing, all-dancing extravaganza every time, so you will notice that there is a Quick & Easy Version at the end of each cake recipe. Each of these begins as a 15cm (6in) round cake. They are then decorated fairly simply with a model or theme taken from the main cake. Don't ever underestimate the power of the ribbon either. It came as a surprise to me to see just how effective different ribbons can be on the same basic cake.

In some of the cakes, such as the Swimming and Golf cakes (see pages 10 and 48) I have used wooden food skewers for certain elements, which I know worries some people. My main reason for this is to get results fast. But, if you prefer everything to be edible, you can substitute raw dried spaghetti or strands of dried gelatine or modelling icing instead. It should also be stressed that the skewers are always visible (never hide cocktail sticks [toothpicks] or skewers inside items, such as figures, that are likely to be eaten) and they should be removed immediately before cutting.

Well, I guess I should go and do some exercise myself now this book is finally finished. (See the Aerobics cake on page 91 for an idea of me at the gym!) Have fun, have a bake and have cake!

Carol Deacon

QUICK & EASY CAKES

The Quick & Easy Version at the end of each main cake is based on a 15cm (6in) round cake on an 18cm (7in) round board. Feel free to alter the size if you wish. You could also use a ready-iced cake from the supermarket if you prefer.

Preparing a sponge cake

Level the cake and turn it upside down. Slice the cake horizontally once or twice and reassemble, filling the layers with jam or buttercream, or a combination of both. Place the cake on the board and spread a coating of jam or buttercream over the sides and top. Place to one side. Dust a work surface with icing (confectioners') sugar and knead 500g (1lb 2oz) white sugarpaste (rolled fondant) until pliable. Roll it out to a thickness of about 5mm (¼in) and lift and place over the cake. Smooth the top and sides with the flats of your hands. For a really professional finish, you can also use a pair of cake smoothers (see Tennis cake on page 51) to iron out any lumps. Then cut away the excess sugarpaste from around the base of the cake.

BASKETBALL

Preparing a fruit cake

You will need to use a 20cm (8in) round cake board to allow for the two coverings. Level the cake and place upside down on the board. Pierce the top a few times with a cocktail stick (toothpick) and drizzle with a couple of tablespoons of brandy. Brush some boiled apricot jam over the top and sides and dust a work surface with icing sugar. Knead 500g (1lb 2oz) marzipan until pliable. (You can soften this in a microwave. Heat on high for 10–15 seconds but don't overheat it or the oil in the marzipan will burn you.) Roll it out and cover the cake. Trim the base and moisten the marzipan with boiled water. Roll out 500g (1lb 2oz) white sugarpaste, as for the sponge cake, and cover the cake again.

BASEBALL

AEROBICS

WATER SPORTS

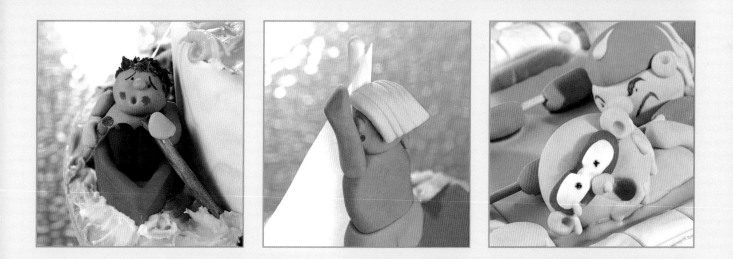

SWIMMING

There is no mistaking the determination on these swimmers' faces!
Personalize the leading swimmer with coloured hair to match the
favourite water baby in your life.

Cake and Decoration

20cm (8in) square sponge (layer) cake
(see page 104)

1 quantity buttercream (see page 106)

Ice blue, black and red food colour pastes

Icing (confectioners') sugar for rolling out

Water for sticking sugarpaste
(rolled fondant)

850g (1lb 14oz) white sugarpaste

150g (5oz) flesh-coloured sugarpaste
(see page 106)

5g (⅛oz) red sugarpaste

60g (2oz) green sugarpaste

20g (¾oz) orange sugarpaste

60g (2oz) pink sugarpaste

½ quantity royal icing (see page 106)

Equipment

25cm (10in) square cake board

Carving knife

Small sharp knife

Cocktail stick (toothpick)

Clean ruler

Fine and medium paintbrushes

2 wooden food skewers (optional)

TIP
*Substitute raw, dried
spaghetti for the skewers,
if preferred.*

1 Level the top of the cake and turn upside down. Slice the cake horizontally into three layers and separate. Cut and discard (or eat!) about a 15cm (6in) square out of the centre of the top layer. Reassemble the cake in the centre of the cake board, sandwiching the layers together with a buttercream filling. Spread a covering of buttercream over the top and sides of the cake.

2 Using a cocktail stick (toothpick), dab a little ice blue food colour into 750g (1lb 10oz) white sugarpaste (rolled fondant). Partially knead to obtain a marbled effect. Dust a work surface with icing (confectioners') sugar and roll out the sugarpaste. Cut a cross into the centre. Lay the sugarpaste over the cake and smooth into position, starting from the top. The cross will splay and tear to allow you to do this. Trim and neaten the base, keeping any excess. To make the tiles, hold and press the edge of a ruler into the icing, first one way and then the other, over the top and sides of the cake. Moisten the cake board

around the base of the cake with a little water. Roll out the leftover marbled sugarpaste and cover the cake board in strips (see Show Jumping cake on page 70). Make lines, as before.

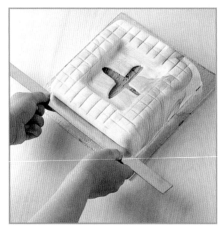

3 To make the front swimmer's body, roll 45g (1½oz) flesh-coloured sugarpaste into a cone (see overleaf). Roll a further 20g (¾oz) sugarpaste into a ball for his head. Using a dab of water, stick on top of the body at a slight angle. Gently push the end of a paintbrush into the bottom of his face and pull down to make a gasping mouth.

4 For the goggles, stick a tiny white oval shape on to a slightly larger red one and stick on to the swimmer's face. Using the end of a paintbrush, pull the centre of the goggles down towards the mouth to make a dip in the centre. Add a tiny flesh-coloured ball for his nose and two for his ears. Poke a small hollow into each ear with a paintbrush and paint two black dots on the eyes. Place the swimmer into position in the pool. Roll

10g (¼oz) flesh-coloured sugarpaste into a sausage for the arms. Cut in half and stick one on the edge of the pool and the other on the side of his body.

5 For the second swimmer, make two 30g (1oz) sugarpaste balls: one green and one flesh-coloured, and slice both balls in half. Assemble the swimmer, using one green half as a body and a flesh half as a head. Stick the other green half on the head to make a cap. Add the features and stick in the pool behind the first swimmer.

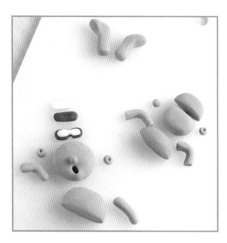

6 To make the legs of the third swimmer, simply roll 30g (1oz) flesh-coloured sugarpaste into a sausage and cut in half. Bend the end of each leg to form an upside-down 'L' shape and stick into position. If you can still see the cake beneath the pool between the swimmers, plug any gaps with leftover sugarpaste.

7 To make the lanes, cut the skewers to length so that they can rest on the sides. (Depending on the width of your pool, this should be about 17cm/6½in). Divide the orange sugarpaste into six and roll into ovals. Thread three on to each skewer and lay them across the pool.

TIP
To check the swimmers are within their lanes, lay the skewers across the pool first.

Stick a small blob of white sugarpaste on top of each end to hold the skewers in place.

8 To make a towel, roll out the remaining green sugarpaste and cut out a rectangle. Press lines into it using the back of a knife and cut a fringe into one end. Partially roll up and stick and drape casually over one edge of the pool. Make a

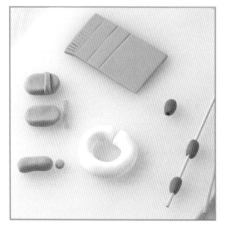

second towel using about 60g (2oz) pink. Use the towels to hide any problem areas!

9 For the rubber rings, divide and roll 60g (2oz) white sugarpaste into two sausages. Slice a sliver off each end and bend into two circles. Stick them in place and paint four red stripes on each with food colour.

QUICK & EASY VERSION
For this cake, make the swimmer as described in the main cake. Partially colour royal icing or buttercream to swirl around the swimmer to look like water.

10 Make the sandals and a shampoo bottle out of the remaining pink sugarpaste. Make two ovals for the sandals and stick a thin strip of pink over each one. For the bottle, make a pink sausage and a tiny ball. Stick the ball on the end of the sausage. Press a few lines into the lid and stick the sandals and shampoo into position on top of the cake. Place about 4 heaped tablespoons of royal icing into a bowl. Stir in about 3–4 tablespoons of water to make it runny. Mix in a little ice blue food colour.

11 Carefully spoon the blue royal icing into the pool, pushing the icing into any awkward areas with a paintbrush as you go. Finally, drip drops of 'water' over both of the swimmers and on to the sides of the pool and the ground.

SCUBA DIVING

Decorating Variation

Cover the cake with pale blue marbled sugarpaste. For the scuba diver, roll out a sausage and split it up the centre. Roll two smaller sausages and a flattish ball for his arms and head.

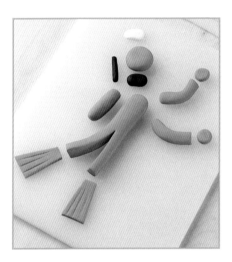

For the diver's mask and breathing pipe, stick one white oval and one black oval on to his face, along with a thin black stick. An orange oval forms his oxygen tank and two flattened discs form his hands. Cut out two flippers and press a few lines on each one with the back of

a knife. Make another two flippers, an arm and a head for the diver on top of the cake plus a triangular black shark's fin.

For the rocks, partially knead together black and white sugarpaste, then pull off little bits and stick them around the cake base.

For the sea, partially mix some ice blue food colour into white royal icing and swirl about the cake top. Pipe green coloured royal icing up the sides to look like seaweed (see Show Jumping cake on page 70). Finally, spoon soft brown sugar around the base of the cake to look like sand.

SURFING

This design uses buttercream to make a magnificent wave. The cake is fairly easy to put together, but if you feel it looks a bit daunting, simply lie the surfer on a flat cake instead.

Cake and Decoration

15cm (6in) square sponge (layer) cake (see page 104)

2 quantities buttercream (see page 106)

Icing (confectioners') sugar for rolling out

Water for sticking sugarpaste (rolled fondant)

60g (2oz) red sugarpaste

120g (4oz) chestnut-coloured sugarpaste

20g (¾oz) purple sugarpaste

20g (¾oz) yellow sugarpaste

Ice blue food colour paste

2–3 teaspoons soft brown sugar

Equipment

Carving knife

20cm (8in) square cake board

Palette knife (metal spatula)

Teaspoon

Pastry brush

Template for surfboard (see page 110)

Ruler

Small sharp knife

Piping tube (tip) or small lid

Paintbrush

1 To transform the square cake into a triangular one, cut a line diagonally through the cake just off-centre. Flip over the smaller section and sit on top of the other so that it forms a triangular shape. Trim away any excess cake to neaten.

2 Slice the two pieces of cake horizontally and fill with buttercream. 'Glue' the two cakes together with another layer of buttercream and stand on the cake board. Spread a thin covering of buttercream around the outside of the cake and, if possible, leave to stand in the refrigerator for a couple of hours. Not only will this stop the cake from moving while decorating it but it should help stop crumbs from getting mixed up in the buttercream covering.

3 Partially colour about 400g (13oz) buttercream blue and, using a palette knife (metal spatula), smear the buttercream all over the cake and the board. Keep back at least 200g (7oz) of the uncoloured buttercream for making the crest of the wave.

4 Using a teaspoon, spoon uncoloured buttercream all along the top edge of the wave. Using a soft brush, such as a pastry brush, stroke the buttercream forwards slightly to form the crest of the wave.

5 Dust a work surface with icing (confectioners') sugar. To make the surfboard, roll out about 60g (2oz) red sugarpaste (rolled fondant) and cut out a board shape. If necessary, use the template on page 110. Gently press into the buttercream on the side of the cake.

> **TIP**
> **If you beat the buttercream very well (5–10 minutes on a moderate speed), it will turn almost white.**

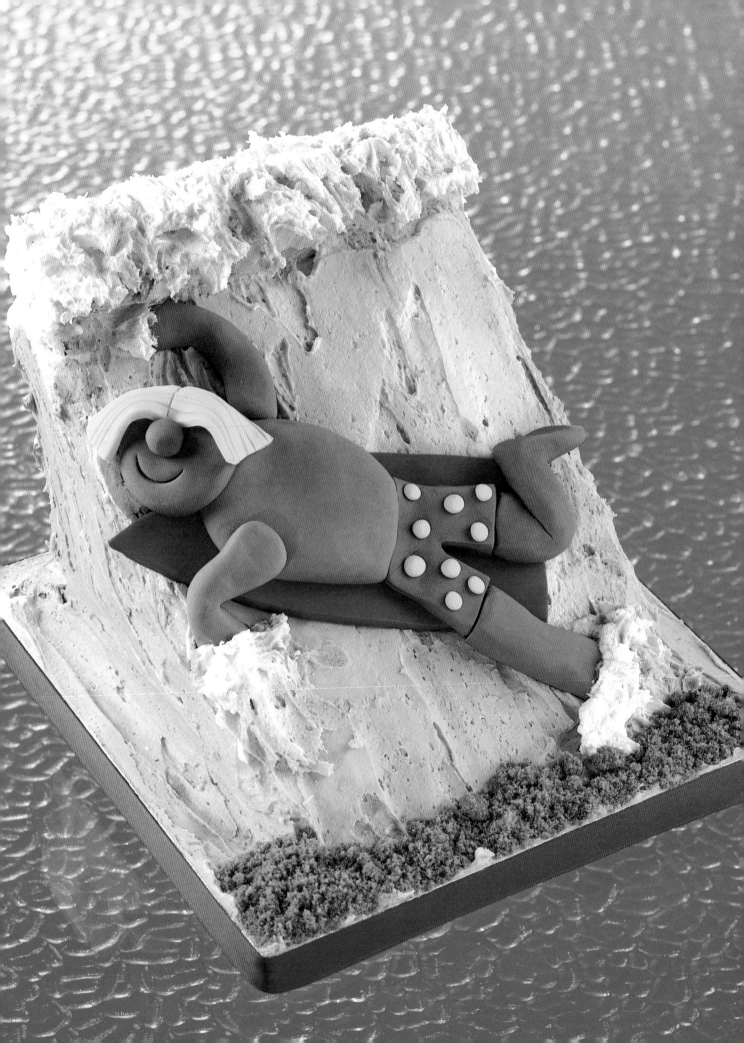

6 To make the surfer, begin with his torso. Roll 45g (1½oz) chestnut-coloured sugarpaste into a flattish oval shape and stick on to the surfboard near the pointed end with a little water.

7 Make two 10g (¼oz) chestnut-coloured sausage shapes for the surfer's arms. Bend both at the elbow and stick on to his torso. See below.

8 Roll out 20g (¾oz) purple sugarpaste and cut out a rectangle for his shorts. Make a cut in the centre of one of the longer sides and splay slightly. Stick on to the board so that the left side just overlaps the edge.

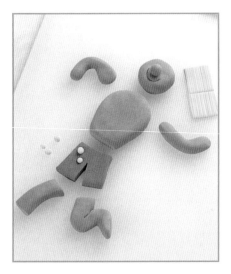

9 Make two 15g (½oz) chestnut-coloured sausage shapes for his legs. Form a flat foot shape in the end of one. Bend it at the knee and stick on to the board. Leave the other one straight.

10 Dab a little of the leftover plain buttercream around the end of each of the surfer's limbs. This will give the effect of the surfer being slightly immersed in the sea (see page 15).

11 Make a 20g (¾oz) chestnut-coloured disc for the surfer's head and stick into position.

12 Press a mouth shape into his face using the edge of something small and rounded, such as a piping tube (tip) or small lid. Stick a small, chestnut-coloured flattened ball just above the smiling mouth for his nose.

13 For the surfer's hair, roll out 20g (¾oz) yellow sugarpaste and lightly press lines into it with the back of a knife. Cut out a small rectangle and lay and stick it over the surfer's head. Press a line into the centre to make a parting.

14 Roll the leftover yellow sugarpaste into nine or ten tiny balls and press and stick all over his shorts.

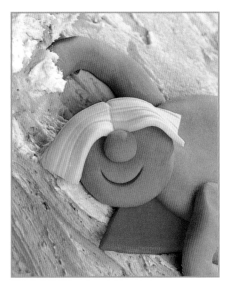

15 Sprinkle 2–3 teaspoons of soft brown sugar along the base of the cake to look like sand.

QUICK & EASY VERSION

Cut out a surfboard shape as before and stick on to the cake. Add two sausage shapes for the surfer's arms and stick as though clutching the board. Add a ball for his head. Press a hollow with the end of a paintbrush for his mouth and add a nose and hair. Smear two-tone buttercream or royal icing sea all around the top of the cake as before. You can use a damp paintbrush to ease the buttercream or royal icing into any awkward corners.

WINDSURFING

Decorating Variation

This version uses an 18cm (7in) round cake on a 20cm (8in) round board. Buttercream and cover the cake using 410g (14oz) white sugarpaste. Make a surfboard as for the main cake and insert a plastic cake dowel through the surfboard and cake to the board below. Measure the height of the protruding dowel and then carefully cut a triangular sail out of rice paper to that measurement. Stick with a little buttercream or royal icing to the mast.

Build the windsurfer from the legs up. Stick two chunky legs on to the board using the mast for support. Remember that you can stick sugarpaste to sugarpaste with water, but you must not get water on the sail or it will dissolve. Make a fairly thin oval shape for his shorts. Slice a little off the top and bottom to flatten slightly and make a cut in the centre. Stick on to the legs. Add a conical shape for the torso and a ball for his head. Make a small hollow with the end of a paintbrush for his mouth and add a ball for his nose. Make two thin sausage shapes for his arms and stick around the sail. Add hair and a two-tone buttercream sea, as on the main cake.

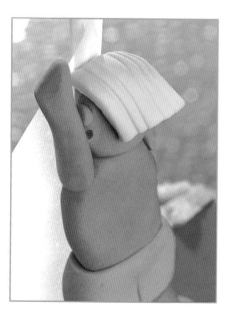

WATER-SKIING

The covered cake board at the back of this cake shows an easy way to provide both a background scene and support for a standing figure. If you feel it looks a little complicated, or you don't have the necessary board to hand, leave it out and simply submerge the water-skier in water, as in the Quick & Easy Version overleaf.

Cake and Decoration

Gelatine or modelling icing (optional) (see page 107)

20cm (8in) round sponge (layer) cake (see page 104)

Icing (confectioners') sugar for rolling out

Water for sticking sugarpaste (rolled fondant)

1 quantity buttercream (see page 106)

1.1kg (2lb 7oz) white sugarpaste

60g (2oz) flesh-coloured sugarpaste (see page 106)

90g (3oz) red sugarpaste

10g (⅓oz) yellow sugarpaste

200g (7oz) green sugarpaste

60g (2oz) black sugarpaste

1 quantity royal icing (see page 106)

Assorted food colour pastes

Equipment

Templates for skis and boat (see page 110)

25cm (10in) thin round cake board

Scalpel or craft knife

Ruler

Carving knife

Palette knife (metal spatula)

30cm (12in) cake board

Rolling pin

Cocktail stick (toothpick)

Fine and medium paintbrushes

Cake smoothers (optional)

Piping bags (see page 107)

1 For three-dimensional skis (see template, page 110), oars and hand bar as shown, use gelatine or modelling icing and leave to dry overnight. Alternatively, use sugarpaste skis, see step 6.

2 Prepare the thin background cake board by slicing about 2.5cm (1in) off one side with a scalpel or craft knife to give it a flat edge on which to stand. Moisten the board with a little water. Dust a work surface with icing (confectioners') sugar and knead and begin to roll out 150g (5oz) white sugarpaste (rolled fondant). Place on to the board and continue to roll out until all the board is covered. Trim and neaten the edges and place to one side to harden.

3 Level the cake and turn upside down. Slice about 2.5cm (1in) vertically off the back of the cake. Split the cake horizontally once or twice and reassemble, sandwiching together with buttercream. Place slightly towards the rear of the main cake board and coat the sides and top with buttercream too.

4 Take 750g (1lb 8oz) white sugarpaste and apply a few dabs of blue food paste on to it with a cocktail stick (toothpick) or clean knife. Lightly knead the colour into the sugarpaste until a marbled effect develops. Roll out the sugarpaste and lift and place over the cake. Smooth into place and neaten the base.

5 Stand the background upright against the back of the cake. Using a pencil, draw a light line on the background level with the top of the cake. This line acts as a guide above which you paint. Paint a simple seascape (see page 108) on the background. Stand it upright behind the cake and stick in place with royal icing.

6 For gelatine or modelling icing skis, place a 15g (½oz) triangle of white sugarpaste on the cake against the background, and stick the ski on top at an angle with a little royal icing. With sugarpaste skis, cut two and lay flat on the surface of the cake.

7 For the skier's front leg, roll 10g (¼oz) flesh-coloured sugarpaste into a thin sausage and bend one end into an 'L' shape for her foot. Bend slightly at the knee and stick the foot on to the ski and the leg against the background with a little water. If using sugarpaste skis, make two legs and stick both in this position.

8 For the skier's swimsuit, roll 10g (¼oz) red sugarpaste into a slightly flattened oval shape and pinch a waist into the middle. Stick against the background.

9 Roll 10g (¼oz) flesh-coloured sugarpaste into a thin sausage for her second leg. Again, make a foot at one end, bend at the knee and gently press and stick with a little water on to the background. The sole of the foot should be flat so as to be able to support the second ski. Pipe a line of royal icing along the edge of the remaining ski and stick on top of the skier's back foot. Add two red straps.

10 Roll 5g (⅛oz) flesh-coloured sugarpaste into a thick disc for the water-skier's head. Paint on facial features with black food colour and add a nose. Stick on to the body.

11 Thinly roll out 5g (⅛oz) yellow sugarpaste for the skier's hair. Press lines into the icing with the back of a knife and cut out a circle. Cut in half and stick the two semicircles on to her head. Stick a tiny ball of red sugarpaste on top and roll the leftover yellow into a pony tail shape. Stick on top of the red and press a few lines into it as before.

12 Carefully tie a length of thread in the centre of the hand bar. Make two arms by rolling 5g (⅛oz) flesh-coloured sugarpaste into a sausage about 6cm (2⅜in) long and cutting it in half. Flatten one end of each arm to make a hand and bend the arms at the elbow.

13 Stick the bar against the body with a little royal icing. Stick the arms against the sides of her body with a little water and bend the hands over the pole as though holding it. Flip the end of the thread over the back of the cake temporarily.

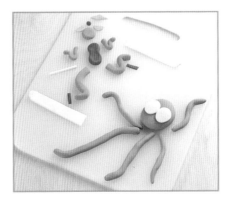

14 To make an octopus, roll 75g (2½oz) green sugarpaste into a conical shape and stick on the main cake board against the side of the cake. Divide and roll 100g (3½oz) green sugarpaste into tentacles and stick on to and around the cake. (See above.)

15 For the boat, lightly roll out 75g (2½oz) red sugarpaste so it is still very thick and cut out a boat shape using the template on page 110. Roll 10g (¼oz) of the remaining red sugarpaste into a thin string and stick around the boat's top.

16 Roll 15g (½oz) green sugarpaste into a ball for the rower's body and stick on the boat. Roll 10g (¼oz) black sugarpaste into a thin string and cut in two for his legs. Bend both legs in half and stick so they fill up the front of the boat.

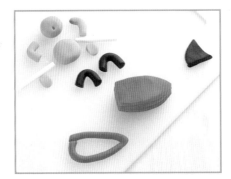

17 Rest the two dried gelatine or modelling icing oars against the side of the boat. Make two tiny green sausage-shaped arms and stick against the rower's body. Stick two tiny flesh-coloured sugarpaste discs on top for his hands.

18 For his head, stick a 10g (¼oz) flesh-coloured ball on his body. Poke a hole for a mouth with the end of a paintbrush and add a nose. Paint the oars with a light brown food colour wash and paint features on both the rower and the octopus. Stir a little brown food colour into a teaspoonful of royal icing and apply with the flat of a knife to the top of his head to give him a wonderful shock of windswept hair.

19 Roll out 45g (1½oz) black sugarpaste fairly thickly and cut out a triangular shark's fin. Re-roll the leftover icing and cut out a second fin. To make the rocks, partially knead the leftover black into 100g (3½oz) white to obtain a marbled effect. Break into pieces and roll into pebble shapes.

20 Place about 6 tablespoons of royal icing or buttercream into a bowl and partially stir in a little blue food colour. Spread and swirl it around the top of the cake and cake board. Stick the rocks, shark's fins and boat in place.

21 Add extra drama with a few waves. Place 1 tablespoon of royal icing or buttercream into a piping bag (with or without a piping tube), fold over the top and cut off the tip. Pipe a short wiggly line on either the cake or board, then stroke and pull

TIP
Candy sticks (sweet cigarettes) or short lengths of drinking straw make ideal ready-made oars and handbars.

backwards with a damp paintbrush to transform into a wave. Repeat all over the cake.

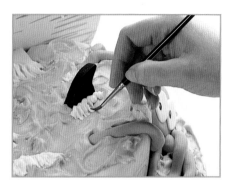

22 Place the loose end of the thread on the back of the boat and stick a small piece of red sugarpaste on top to hold in place.

23 Pipe a line of royal icing or buttercream dots around the edge of the background board to hide the edge. You can leave it plain if you prefer.

QUICK & EASY VERSION

This very quick version consists of just a head, hands, bar and skis but would still make a water-skiing recipient smile! If you don't want to make gelatine or modelling icing skis (or if you are short of time), substitute shorter, stockier sugarpaste ones.

SKIING

Decorating Variation

Cut, cover and paint a 20cm (8in) thin cake board as for the main cake. Then carve an irregular snow-scene shape into a 20cm (8in) round cake. Cover it with buttercream and dampen the board around the cake with a little water. Cover both the cake and board all in one go with 750g (1lb 8oz) white sugarpaste.

Make the skis out of gelatine or modelling icing, then dry and paint red. Alternatively, use sugarpaste ones. Make the skier's ski suit all in one piece (see the scuba diver on page 25). His ski poles are strands of spaghetti with black sugarpaste discs on the ends. Position and paint black with food colour paste.

Stick white sugarpaste snowballs around the cake. A little white royal icing piped and pulled (as main cake) gives the effect of snowdrifts. Daub pale blue food colour around the scene and sieve icing sugar over the cake.

SAILING

When painting food colour on to marzipan, a lovely streaky, woodgrain effect is obtained, as you can see on the boat sides and seats. For those who dislike marzipan, substitute sugarpaste.

Cake and Decoration

1 sponge (layer) cake baked in 1kg (2lb) loaf tin (pan) (see page 104)

1 quantity buttercream (see page 106)

Icing (confectioners') sugar for rolling out

Water for sticking sugarpaste (rolled fondant)

75g (2½oz) black sugarpaste

410g (13oz) white marzipan

60g (2oz) blue sugarpaste

80g (2¾oz) orange sugarpaste

60g (2oz) white sugarpaste

90g (3oz) flesh-coloured sugarpaste (see page 106)

Brown, black and blue food colour pastes

1 sheet rice paper

1 strand raw dried spaghetti

1 quantity royal icing (optional) (see page 106)

Equipment

Carving knife

25cm (10in) square cake board

Palette knife (metal spatula)

Rolling pin

Small sharp knife

Fine and medium paintbrushes

1 plastic cake dowel (available from cake decorating shops)

Piping bags (see page 107)

Scissors

Any piping tube (tip)

1 Level the top of the cake and cut the front into a point. Slice in half horizontally and fill with a layer of buttercream. Place the cake diagonally on the cake board and spread a layer of buttercream around the sides and top.

2 Dust the work surface with icing (confectioners') sugar and thinly roll out about 75g (2½oz) black sugarpaste (rolled fondant). Lay on top of the boat. Trim it to the edge of the cake and peel away any excess.

3 Roll out 60g (2oz) marzipan and cut out two thin strips for the seats in the boat. Lay and stick them across the boat.

4 Measure the height and circumference of the boat. Add a couple of millimetres on to the height, roll out 350g (12oz) marzipan and cut out a strip.

5 Run a knife along under the marzipan strip to make sure it is not stuck to the work

surface and roll up the strip like a loose bandage. Holding it vertically, unwind it around the sides of the cake.

6 Trim and neaten the join and the base and press a few horizontal lines around the sides of the boat to look like planks of wood. Paint both the sides and the seats of the boat with some watered-down brown food colour.

7 For the mast, stick a plastic cake dowel vertically through the cake until it reaches the board beneath. Cut a triangle of rice paper for the sail and stick to the mast with royal icing or buttercream.

8 For the sailor, roll 60g (2oz) blue sugarpaste into a sausage shape for his trousers. Bend into a horseshoe and stick on to the boat with a little water. The ends should just dangle over the sides. Make two 5g (⅙oz) white balls for his turn-ups and squash each into a flattish disc. Stick one on the end of each trouser leg. (See below and page 12.)

9 Roll 75g (2½oz) orange sugarpaste into a disc for the sailor's life jacket and press lines down the front with the back of a knife. Stick it on to the trousers and insert a strand of spaghetti down the centre to provide extra support.

10 Roll 15g (½oz) flesh-coloured sugarpaste into a ball for his head. Slot on to the spaghetti and stick on to the body. Roll 45g (1½oz) flesh-coloured sugarpaste into a sausage shape for his legs. Cut in half and stick one end to the trousers and the other on to the board.

11 Make three small flesh-coloured balls. Stick two on the sides of the head for ears and the other in the centre of the face for his nose. Push a small hollow into each ear with the end of a paintbrush.

12 Roll 30g (1oz) flesh-coloured sugarpaste into a sausage for his arms. Cut in half and stick one on so that the hand rests on his head and the other so that the hand rests in his lap. Place a little black royal icing or buttercream into a piping bag, snip off the end and pipe a wiggly beard on his face and hair on his head.

13 To make a gull, first roll 15g (½oz) white sugarpaste into a sausage shape. Squeeze lightly just below one end to form a head and tweak the other end into a point for its

QUICK & EASY VERSION

If you would prefer your sailor rowing, there is a rower on the base of the Water-Skiing cake on page 19. This one uses the boat base template on page 110 and a candy stick or drinking straw as a mast. A triangle of rice paper makes a great sail, and a simple model looks out to sea. Make his buttons by pressing the end of a drinking straw into the icing to leave little circles. Here, the sea is simply watered-down blue food colour painted on the cake surface.

tail. Pinch a beak shape into the head and bend the head upwards slightly. Make three gulls. Stick one in the boat and the others on the board. For the fish, make two tiny orange triangles. Press a curved line for a mouth using the edge of a piping tube (tip) or small lid and paint a few scales and eyes with some black food colour. Also, paint two dots for eyes on the sailor and add eyes and markings on the birds.

14 Place 4 tablespoons royal icing or buttercream into a bowl and partially mix in a little blue food colour to give a mottled effect. Smear the sea around the boat.

15 Place a little white royal icing or plain buttercream into a piping bag and fold over the top a couple of times. Snip a small triangle off the end and pipe wiggly lines on the waves. Using a damp paintbrush, draw the icing towards you to make waves (see Water-skiing cake on page 18).

TIP
You will be able to find packs of 'writing icing' at the supermarket. These tubes of ready-coloured icing are ideal for small tasks like hair.

ROWING

Decorating Variation

This cake is again made out of a loaf tin (pan) cake and placed on a 30cm (12in) round cake board. Cut the cake into a boat shape as for the sailing boat, using the two cutaway corners to form a second point at the rear of the boat. Because it is longer, you will need to use slightly more marzipan to go around the sides of the boat (about 500g/1lb 2oz).

The rowers are very simple to make. A conical shape forms each torso, two sausage shapes bent in half form their legs and another two their arms. The secret of this cake is to fill the top of the boat as much as possible. On this design, the oars are simply sections of cut-down drinking straws, but you could substitute gelatine or modelling icing oars if you prefer everything on the cake to be edible (see recipes on page 107).

The cox sits the other way round. He has a cap on his head and holds a megaphone in his hands. To make the water a little different, this time two colours were partially mixed into the icing: mint green and ice blue.

TEAM SPORTS

BASKETBALL

Use these players as a guide, dressing them in the colours of your favourite team. Feel free to add hair, pot bellies or anything else that takes your fancy. Personalize them to look like your favourite birthday basketball player.

Cake and Decoration

2 quantities buttercream (see page 106)

3 tablespoons cocoa powder

3 tablespoons hot water

18cm (7in) square sponge (layer) cake (see page 104) (trim down a 20cm/8in cake if necessary)

Icing (confectioners') sugar for rolling out

Water for sticking sugarpaste (rolled fondant)

60g (2oz) white sugarpaste

90g (3oz) brown sugarpaste

60g (2oz) blue sugarpaste

60g (2oz) pink sugarpaste

30g (1oz) flesh-coloured sugarpaste (see page 106)

20g (¾oz) orange sugarpaste

Black food colour paste

30g (1oz) grey-coloured desiccated (shredded) coconut (see page 109)

Equipment

20cm (8in) square cake board

Carving knife

Small sharp knife

Plastic cake dowel (available from cake decorating shops)

Paintbrush

Wooden food skewer (optional)

Piping tube (tip) or small lid

15cm (6in) square of aluminium foil

Small section of net (use either tulle or a net used to hold oranges)

Scissors

1 First mix up the chocolate buttercream. Make the basic buttercream mixture and then mix together the cocoa powder and hot water to make a paste. Beat into the buttercream.

2 Stand the cake on its side. If it leans or wobbles, slice a little away to enable it to stand up securely. Cut the cake into three or four slices. Reassemble diagonally on the cake board, spreading a layer of buttercream between the layers. For extra security, you can push a plastic cake dowel (which has been cut to the same length as the height of the cake) through the cake.

3 Gently hold the top of the cake and spread a thick layer of chocolate buttercream around the sides. When completed, buttercream the top as well. Using something like the end of a paintbrush or a wooden food skewer, draw a brick pattern into the buttercream.

4 To make the big player, begin with his feet (see page 30). Make two 20g (¾oz) white sugarpaste (rolled fondant) 'L' shapes and stick against the bottom centre of the wall. Dab a little water on the top of the ankle of each boot and roll 20g (¾oz) brown sugarpaste into a sausage about 12cm (6in) long. Cut in half and slice a little off the outer ends to neaten. Bend slightly at the knees and stick into position, gently pressing into the buttercream wall.

5 To make the shorts, roll 10g (¼oz) blue sugarpaste into a sausage and cut in half. Slice a little off the rounded end of each half

TIP
If the buttercream loses its adhesive properties, 'rough it up' slightly with the tip of a paintbrush or cocktail stick (toothpick) where you want to stick something.

sausage to form a sort of rectangle. Dab a little water on the top of each leg and stick the shorts into position. Dab a little water on the top of the shorts ready for the body.

6 For the body, shape about 20g (¾oz) pink sugarpaste into a flattish triangular shape. The neck should be level with the top of the cake. Stick into position. For the head, make two 15g (½oz) balls, one in blue and one in brown. Slice about a third off each and discard the smaller portions. Pinch and pull the flat base of the blue to form the brim of the baseball cap. Stick it on to the brown to form the head. Using something small and circular, such as a piping tube (tip) or a small lid, press a semicircle into the icing to leave a smile. Stick on top of the cake and add tiny brown balls of sugarpaste for his nose and ears.

Quick & Easy Version

Make the player after the ribbon has been put around the base, positioning him so that his legs dangle over the side. Just to emphasize what sport he is into, surround him with plenty of basketballs.

7 To make the smaller player behind, stick two 5g (⅛oz) white sugarpaste ovals on to the board for feet. Roll 5g (⅛oz) flesh-coloured sugarpaste into a sausage and cut in half for his legs. Stick on to the feet. Roll and cut a 10g (¼oz) pink sugarpaste sausage in half for the shorts and stick on to the legs. Roll and flatten a 10g (¼oz) sausage of blue sugarpaste into a triangle for the body and stick into position. Roll 5g (⅛oz) flesh-coloured sugarpaste into a sausage and cut in half for arms. Gently stick them to the body.

8 Flatten a 5g (⅛oz) ball of flesh-coloured sugarpaste into a thick disc for the head and press the icing tube into it to leave a glum expression. Stick on top of the body. Roll 10g (¼oz) brown sugarpaste into a sausage for the tall player's arm. Flatten one end to form the hand and stick in position, resting the hand on the head of the player standing behind him. Finish off the smaller player with a nose, two ears and arms.

9 Make the second short player in exactly the same way up until the head. To make him appear to be looking up, stick a small brown ball and two flattened white balls on the top of his head. Stick an ear on either side of the head and a small sausage on either side of the body for his arms. Using black food colour and a fine paintbrush, paint some hair on the head, two dots on the eyes and sports shoe markings on all the boots.

10 For the net, roll a little foil into a stick. Cut out a section of orange net and thread the foil through. Twist the ends together. Roll the orange sugarpaste into a ball and press a few lines into it with a knife. Position the net and place the ball on top to hold it in place. Roll 10g (¼oz) brown sugarpaste into an arm, and stick on, holding the ball. Moisten the board, or cover with buttercream, and sprinkle with coloured coconut.

NETBALL

Decorating Variation

Build and cover the basic cake as for the main one. The netball post is a plastic cake dowel. Stand one end in a ball of white sugarpaste and press into the side of the cake. Make a net and ball as for the main cake. Place the net on top of the post and the ball on top of the tail of the net. The girls have oval feet, and socks made out of small discs with lines made using the back of a knife. Their skirts are slightly flared rectangles with lines pressed into them with the end of a paintbrush to give the effect of pleats (see Armchair Supporter cake on page 88). Their hair is piped buttercream, but you could use sugarpaste if you prefer.

BASEBALL

The batter and catcher from opposing teams glower at each other across the top of the cake. Of course, you could make them happy by simply making their mouths the other way up. To personalize the cake, dress the players in your favourite team's colours.

Cake and Decoration

20cm (8in) round sponge (layer) cake (see page 104)

1 quantity buttercream (see page 106)

Icing (confectioners') sugar for rolling out

Water for sticking sugarpaste (rolled fondant)

1kg (2lb 4oz) white sugarpaste

90g (3oz) red sugarpaste

60g (2oz) blue sugarpaste

45g (1½oz) flesh-coloured sugarpaste (see page 106)

10g (¼oz) brown sugarpaste

45g (1½oz) black sugarpaste

2 strands raw dried spaghetti

Black, red and green food colour pastes

30g (1oz) green-coloured desiccated (shredded) coconut (see page 109)

2 tablespoons royal icing (optional) (see page 106)

Equipment

Carving knife

25cm (10in) round cake board

Rolling pin

Small sharp knife

Cake smoothers (optional)

No. 2 or 3 piping tube (tip) or small lid (optional)

Fine and medium paintbrushes

Piping bag (optional) (see page 107)

70cm (27in) ribbon

Adhesive tape (optional)

1 Level the top of the cake and turn upside down. Split it horizontally into layers and fill with buttercream. Reassemble and place in the middle of the cake board. Spread buttercream all over.

2 Knead 750g (1lb 8oz) white sugarpaste (rolled fondant) until pliable. Dust a work surface with icing (confectioners') sugar and roll out the sugarpaste to a thickness of about 7mm (¼in). Lift and place over the top of the cake. Ease it into position and smooth the top and sides. Trim away any excess.

3 Moisten the cake board with a little water. Roll out 200g (7oz) white sugarpaste and cut a strip about 84cm (33in) long. Slice away a little icing from one edge to neaten it and slide your knife along under the strip to prevent sticking.

4 Carefully roll up the icing like a bandage and unwind around the base of the cake making sure that the neat cut edge is the one up against the cake itself. Smooth, trim and neaten the edges and join.

5 To make the batter, start with his trousers. Roll 60g (2oz) white sugarpaste into a sausage about 18cm (7in) long. Bend into a horseshoe shape and stick on the cake.

6 Roll 60g (2oz) red sugarpaste into a conical shape for his body and sit on top of his legs. For extra security, insert a strand of spaghetti through the body, leaving 2cm (¾in) protruding to fix his head onto.

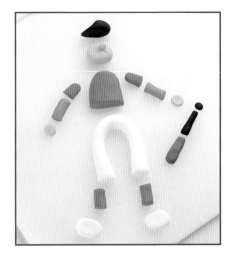

7 Make two small 10g (¼oz) red sausage shapes for the lower part of his legs and stick on to the trousers. Make two 10g (¼oz) white oval shapes for his feet and stick on to the ends of his legs.

8 To make the batter's shirt sleeves, roll 10g (¼oz) red sugarpaste into an oval, then cut in half. Stick either side of his body. For lower arms, roll 10g (¼oz) blue sugarpaste into a sausage and cut in half. Stick in position.

9 Roll 15g (½oz) flesh-coloured sugarpaste into a ball for his head and slot and stick on to the sugarpaste. Holding a piping tube (tip) or small lid, press a downwards curving mouth. Alternatively, paint a mouth using a little black food colour.

10 For the bat, make two small tapering sausage shapes; one brown, one black. (The brown should be slightly larger.) Slice a little off the thinnest end of the brown and the widest end of the black and splice. Stick the bat against the batter's body. Stick two flesh-coloured hands at the base of the bat, and a nose on his face.

11 For his cap, roll 10g (¼oz) black sugarpaste into a semicircle. Pinch and pull one side into a brim and stick on his head pointing backwards. Paint fine black food colour lines down his legs.

12 To make the catcher, again begin with his legs. Roll 45g (1½oz) white sugarpaste into a sausage about 18cm (7in) long. Bend into a horseshoe shape and stick on to the cake. Roll 45g (1½oz) white icing into a cone for his body and stick on to the body. Insert spaghetti, as before.

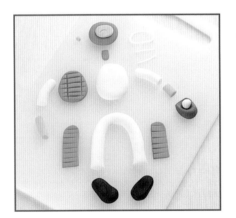

13 Make the leg protectors by rolling 15g (½oz) blue sugarpaste into a sausage about 10cm (4in) long. Flatten slightly and cut in half. Press lines across the width of each pad using the back of a knife. Stick one on top of each leg.

QUICK & EASY VERSION
This cake has just one of the characters sitting on the top. In this case he is smiling – presumably because it's his birthday and he's the best!

14 For the chest plate, mould 15g (½oz) blue sugarpaste into a flat triangle. Press lines across the pad with a knife and two vertical ones down its length. Stick on his chest. Roll 20g (¾oz) blue sugarpaste into a ball for his head and stick on the body.

15 To make the sleeves, roll 15g (½oz) white sugarpaste into a sausage about 6cm (2½in) long. Cut in half and stick against the sides of his body. Roll 5g (⅙oz) flesh-coloured sugarpaste into a sausage for the arms. Cut in two and stick into position. Make a slightly flat triangular shape for his face and stick on to the front of his helmet. Press in a mouth as before.

16 For the helmet, roll and stick two tiny white sugarpaste string shapes across the front of his face and a longer one around the edge of the face. The join should lie at the base where it can be hidden. Cut out a tiny flat blue arched shape for his throat protector and stick on to the bottom of his face. Finish his face with a small ball for a nose.

17 For the glove, roll 5g (⅙oz) brown sugarpaste into a thick oval. Slice a little off one end and press a hollow in the centre. Stick on his arm. Roll some leftover white sugarpaste into a ball and stick inside his mitt. Make two 10g (¼oz) black ovals for feet and stick on the legs. Paint a red stripe on the ball.

18 To make the grass, place 30g (1oz) desiccated (shredded) coconut into a bowl and add colouring, as on page 109. Spread a thin covering of buttercream or royal icing around the players and, using a teaspoon, sprinkle the coconut around them. Use a paintbrush to push the grass into any awkward areas.

19 Place about 1 tablespoon royal icing into a piping bag fitted with a no. 2 or 3 piping tube and pipe a line of dots or a 'snail trail'. Squeeze a little icing out of the bag, release the pressure, pull slightly so the icing forms a tail, then squeeze and release again around the base of the cake. Stick the ribbon around the side.

CRICKET

'Owzat!' – or maybe I should say 'Owzis?' – for a cake to bowl them over with. This two-tiered design is actually much easier to put together than it looks and it means you could have two different flavoured cakes. Of course, it would work just as well using one cake – simply stand or sit the batsman next to the bowler.

1 Level the tops of both cakes and turn upside down. Slice horizontally into two or three layers and sandwich together with buttercream. Place the smaller cake on to the small thin cake board and the larger one towards the rear of the bigger cake board. Buttercream around the sides and top of both cakes.

2 Cover the smaller cake using 400g (14oz) white sugarpaste (rolled fondant). Smooth the sides and trim and neaten the base. The board too should be hidden. Cover the larger one with 750g (1lb 10oz) white sugarpaste. Measure the height of the larger cake and cut the cake dowels to that measurement. Insert them in a triangular formation just off-centre. (Cake dowels prevent the top cake from squashing the lower one.)

3 Place a small dab of royal icing or buttercream on the top of the larger cake and stand the smaller one on top in the centre. Don't worry if the cake does not sit absolutely flush all the way round.

4 To decorate the top tier, first roll 5g (⅙oz) brown sugarpaste into a long thin string and cut into three equal-length stumps and a shorter length for the bails. Stick them against the side of the cake with a little water and press a few lines in the bails with the back of a knife.

5 Make two 5g (⅙oz) white sugarpaste ovals for the batsman's feet and stick them pointing in the same direction next to the stumps. To make the legs, roll 30g (1oz) white sugarpaste into a sausage about 10cm (4in) long and cut in half. Bend each leg slightly at the knee and stick against the side of the cake. Roll out about 15g (½oz) white sugarpaste and cut out two arched shapes for pads. Press a few lines down each one with the back of a knife and stick on to the front of the legs. Cut out a thin rectangle to make a strap for the rear leg and stick in place.

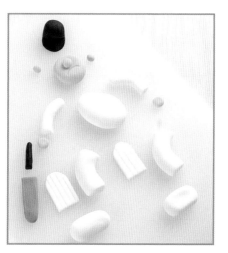

Cake and Decoration

15cm (6in) round sponge (layer) cake (see page 104)

20cm (8in) round sponge cake (see page 104)

2 quantities buttercream (see page 106)

Icing (confectioners') sugar for rolling out

Water for sticking sugarpaste (rolled fondant)

1.4kg (3lb 1oz) white sugarpaste

15g (½oz) brown sugarpaste

15g (½oz) black sugarpaste

60g (2oz) flesh-coloured sugarpaste (see page 106)

5g (⅙oz) red sugarpaste

1 quantity royal icing (optional) (see page 106)

Ice blue, mint green and black food colour pastes

1 strand raw dried spaghetti

45g (1½oz) green-coloured desiccated (shredded) coconut (see page 109)

Equipment

Carving knife

15cm (6in) thin round cake board

25cm (10in) round cake board

Rolling pin

Cake smoothers (optional)

Small sharp knife

3 plastic cake dowels (available from cake decorating specialists)

Serrated knife

Piping tube (tip) or small lid

Piping bag (see page 107)

6 Roll 20g (¾oz) white icing into an oval for his body. Press and stick it on top of the legs and against the side of the cake. It should lean forwards slightly. Insert a small strand of spaghetti to provide extra support. Make a 10g (¼oz) sausage shape, also in white, for the arms and cut in half. Bend at the elbows and stick in position.

7 Roll 15g (½oz) flesh-coloured sugarpaste into a ball for his head and stick on top of the body. Press a glum-looking mouth into his face using the edge of a piping tube (tip) or small lid. Stick three small, flesh-coloured balls on to the face for his ears and nose. Roll the remaining black sugarpaste into a semicircular shape for his cap and pinch and pull the front forwards slightly. Stick on his head.

8 To make the bat, roll 5g (⅛oz) brown sugarpaste into a small sausage shape, then flatten slightly. Slice a little off one end and lay and stick against his legs. Stick a tiny strip of black above the brown for a handle and then position two small flesh-coloured sugarpaste balls on top for his hands.

9 To make the bowler, first roll 20g (¾oz) white sugarpaste into an oval for his body. Lay and stick on to the board. Make two 10g (¼oz) sausage shapes for his arms and stick into position. Roll 30g (1oz) white into a sausage for his legs and cut in half. Stick next to each other on the

QUICK & EASY VERSION

Begin this simple-to-make cricketer with a sausage of sugarpaste (rolled fondant) bent into a horseshoe shape for legs. Add a ball for his body and two oval shapes for his feet. The head, helmet and arms are made as for the main cake. Add a bat and ball, then daub watery green food colour around the top to look like grass. You could also add hair or anything else to make it look like your favourite batsman.

board. Make two 10g (¼oz) oval shapes for his shoes and stick one on the end of each leg.

10 Roll 15g (½oz) flesh-coloured sugarpaste into a ball for his head. Press and stick on to the body. Give him a happy, upturned smile with the piping tube or lid. Also make three flesh-coloured sugarpaste ball shapes for his ears and nose and two slightly larger ones for his hands, and stick into position. Roll the red sugarpaste into a ball and stick on to the outstretched hand. To make the bowler's hair, stick a small strip of brown sugarpaste on top of his head

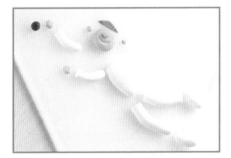

and press lines into it with the back of a knife. Also poke a line of stitching in the ball with the tip of the knife.

11 Paint a few simple clouds on the sides of the cake with ice blue food colour, and two dots on the fielder's eyes with black.

12 Colour 2 tablespoons of royal icing or buttercream green and place in a piping bag. Fold over the end of the bag a couple of times to close and cut a tiny V-shape or tiny triangle off the pointed end. Pipe simple leaf shapes around the edges and bases of both cakes. To do this, squeeze a little icing out of the bag on to the cake, release the pressure from your fingers and pull away.

13 Colour 45g (1½oz) desiccated (shredded) coconut green (see page 109). Spread buttercream around the board and cover with coconut to look like grass. Sprinkle a little on the cake top.

BOWLS

I had not realized just how popular bowling was until I began putting this book together and found out how many people play it. If you do not want to carve up a square cake, you could use a rectangular cake baked in a loaf tin instead.

Cake and Decoration

15cm (6in) square sponge (layer) cake (see page 104)

½ quantity buttercream (see page 106)

Icing (confectioners') sugar for rolling out

600g (1lb 5oz) pale green sugarpaste

225g (8oz) white sugarpaste

Water for sticking sugarpaste (rolled fondant)

60g (2oz) flesh-coloured sugarpaste (see page 106)

30g (1oz) black sugarpaste

1 strand raw dried spaghetti

1 tablespoon royal icing (optional) (see page 106)

Green and black food colour pastes

45g (1½oz) green-coloured desiccated (shredded) coconut (see page 109)

Equipment

Carving knife

25cm (10in) round cake board

Rolling pin

Cake smoothers (optional)

Small sharp knife

No. 3 piping tube (tip) or small lid

Fine and medium paintbrushes

Piping bag (see page 107)

Scissors

1 To turn the square cake into a rectangular one, level the top and turn upside down. Slice 5cm (2in) off one side and lay against one of the shorter sides of the remaining cake. Trim the excess to form a 10 x 20cm (4 x 8in) rectangle. Then slice the cake horizontally into one or two layers and sandwich together with buttercream. Place the cake in position in the centre of the cake board and cover the top and sides with buttercream.

2 Dust a work surface with icing (confectioners') sugar and knead and roll out all the pale green-coloured sugarpaste (rolled fondant). Lift and place over the top of the cake and smooth into position. Trim and neaten the base.

3 To make the bowler, make two 10g (¼oz) white sugarpaste oval shapes for the shoes and two 30g (1oz) white sugarpaste sausage shapes about 7cm (3in) long for legs (see above right). Bend both the legs into right angles.

4 Position one leg with the lower half flat on the cake. The other should be next to it facing forwards and with the knee bent. Place one shoe under the front leg and the other behind the back leg at an angle. Stick everything in place and push a strand of spaghetti through the back leg into the cake to provide extra support. Leave 5cm (2in) protruding.

ICE HOCKEY

The goal adds a nice touch to this design, but you can leave it out if you don't have time to make one. Sit the player in the middle of the cake instead, to fill up the extra space. Dress him in the colours of the recipient's favourite team.

Cake and Decoration

1 quantity gelatine or modelling icing (optional) (see page 107) or 6 candy sticks (sweet cigarettes)

15cm (6in) square sponge (layer) cake (see page 104)

½ quantity buttercream (see page 106)

Icing (confectioners') sugar for rolling out

Water for sticking sugarpaste (rolled fondant)

650g (1lb 7oz) white sugarpaste

150g (5oz) red sugarpaste

30g (1oz) dark blue sugarpaste

30g (1oz) flesh-coloured sugarpaste (see page 106)

60g (2oz) black sugarpaste

5g (⅛oz) grey sugarpaste

10g (¼oz) pale blue sugarpaste

1 strand raw dried spaghetti

1 quantity royal icing (see page 106)

Black, blue and red food colour pastes

Equipment

Carving knife

20cm (8in) square cake board

Rolling pin

Small sharp knife

Cake smoothers (optional)

Orange net or tulle

Scissors

Piping bags (see page 107)

Nos. 1 and 2 piping tubes (tips)

Small lid (optional)

Fine and medium paintbrushes

1 You can make the goal posts out of either gelatine or modelling icing. Make at least eight thin stick shapes (to allow for breakages), each of which are 5cm (2in) long, and leave to dry. Candy sticks or sweet cigarettes make excellent ready-made alternatives.

2 Also make a couple of longer strands and bend one end of each into a curve to make simple hockey sticks. Again, leave to dry. Alternatively, you can make sugarpaste (rolled fondant) sticks instead. However, as they will not be as strong as gelatine ones, stick them flat on the top of the cake and alter the position of the player's arms when you come to stick them in place.

3 Level the top of the cake and turn upside down. Slice in half horizontally and fill with buttercream. Reassemble and place on to the cake board. Spread a covering of buttercream over the top and sides.

4 Dust a work surface with icing (confectioners') sugar and knead and roll out 500g (1lb 2oz) white sugarpaste. Lift and place over the cake and smooth into position. Trim and neaten the base.

5 With a little water, moisten the exposed cake board around the base of the cake. Knead and roll out 100g (3½oz) red sugarpaste and cut out four strips. Lay one along each of the four sides (see Show Jumping cake on page 70). Make

a diagonal cut at each corner and peel away the excess icing. Trim and neaten the sides of the board.

6 Once dry, assemble the goal. Stick the two front posts into small balls of white sugarpaste. Stand them on the cake a stick-width apart and secure with a dab of royal icing. Lean another stick diagonally behind each front one and a fifth one either behind or just in front of these two on the cake itself. Finally, lay one across the top of the goal. Stick them all in place with royal icing.

7 Cut a small rectangle out of an orange net or some tulle. Pipe some royal icing along the

> **TIP**
> *For a simpler goal, copy the one on the field hockey variation cake instead (page 45).*

tops and sides of the posts and press and stick the netting into place. Roll about 10g (¼oz) red sugarpaste into a long thin string and gently press and stick with royal icing around the mouth of the goal to hide the ends of the net.

8 To make the player, start with his legs. Roll 30g (1oz) blue sugarpaste into a sausage and bend into a horseshoe shape and stick on to the edge of the cake with a little water. Position with one leg dangling over the side. Roll 100g (3½oz) white sugarpaste into an oval for his body and stick on top of the legs. Insert a strand of spaghetti for extra support. Leave about 2.5cm (1in) protruding on which to slot his head.

QUICK & EASY VERSION

This player demonstrates how a sugarpaste hockey stick can be just as effective as a 3-D one made from gelatine or modelling icing. The stick lies flat on the cake with the player's hand holding it in place. He has also been daubed with some brown food colour, as well as green. This gives the impression of his having been involved in a very muddy game.

9 Roll 15g (½oz) flesh-coloured sugarpaste into an oval for his head and stick on to the body. Press a smile into his face using the edge of a piping tube (tip) or small lid.

10 Mould about 10g (¼oz) red sugarpaste into a semicircular shape for his helmet and stick on top of his head. Press a couple of lines in the top with the back of a knife. Thinly roll out 10g (¼oz) red and cut out a thin strip about 7cm (2½in) long. Lay and stick around the player's head, just below the base of the helmet.

11 Make three tiny flesh-coloured balls for the ice hockey player's features. Stick two on the sides of his head for his

ears and one in the centre of his face for his nose. Push a small hollow into each ear with the end of a paintbrush.

12 To make the boots, roll two 20g (¾oz) lumps of black sugarpaste into 'L' shapes and stick one on the end of each leg. Roll out about 5g (⅙oz) grey sugarpaste and cut out two thin rectangles. Stick one on the base of each boot for blades.

13 Roll 30g (1oz) white sugarpaste into a sausage for his arms and cut in half. Stick them in place against the body. If using a gelatine or modelling icing hockey stick, glue the stick against the chest with a little royal icing and hold in place with two small flesh-coloured sugarpaste ovals for hands. If using a sugarpaste hockey stick, lay it flat on the cake and stick one arm against the side of the body with the hand positioned on top of the stick.

14 Decorate the player's strip (see above right). Using a piping tube as a cutter, cut out and stick three flat pale blue sugarpaste discs on his chest. Stick a couple of red squares on his shoulders. Paint lines with black food colour down his sleeves and two black rectangles on his skate blades to give the impression of their being cut out. Paint the handle of the hockey stick black.

15 Place a no. 1 or 2 piping tube (tip) in a piping bag and pipe white royal icing laces on to the boots. Pipe a 'snail trail' around the base of the cake. To do this, squeeze a little icing out of the tube, release the pressure, keeping the tip of the tube still in the icing. Pull it along the base of the cake slightly to form a tail and then squeeze another blob out of the tube. Repeat this 'squeeze, release' action all around the cake. Alternatively, leave plain or just pipe dots instead.

16 Paint a few watery blue streaks diagonally across the cake to give the impression of ice. Stick a small black sugarpaste disc on the cake for the puck.

17 Place about 1 tablespoon of red-coloured royal icing into a piping bag fitted with a no. 2 piping tube and pipe a red line along each edge of the cake. Gently brush away icing sugar marks with a damp paintbrush and leave the cake to dry.

HOCKEY

Decorating Variation

The cake and board are the same size as for the main cake. The goal posts on this version are far easier to make as they consist of only three gelatine or modelling icing posts, or candy sticks (sweet cigarettes). Two posts are stuck into sugarpaste balls and the third is laid across the top and glued into place with a little royal icing. Alternatively, leave out the goal post completely! Cover the board with green sugarpaste rather than the red that is used in the main cake.

To make the player, start with a white oval for her body. Cut out a flat red rectangle for the bib and cut a semicircle out of the top edge. Stick on to the body and push some spaghetti through the centre for support. Make two long flesh-coloured sausage shapes for her legs and stick into position. Add two red sugarpaste ovals for socks and black ones for boots. Press a couple of lines into the socks to look like creases.

Cut out a black rectangle for the hockey player's skirt and press lines into it using a paintbrush to give the impression of pleats. Drape and stick over the top of her legs.

Make a flesh-coloured ball for her head. Press a smile with the edge of a piping tube and add a tiny flesh-coloured dot for her nose and paint two black dots for eyes. Roll out some yellow sugarpaste for hair. Press lines

into it with the back of a knife. Cut a circle and slice in half. Stick on the head.

Place the hockey stick into position and hold in place with two flesh-coloured sausage-shaped arms. Paint the handle of the stick with black food colour and the rest of the stick with brown. Alternatively, if using a sugarpaste stick, lay it flat on the cake and alter the positions of the arms.

Daub some watered-down green food colour over the top of the cake and make some grass by pushing leftover green sugarpaste through a sieve (see Golf cake on page 48). Pipe a 'snail trail' around the base of the cake, as on the main design, or colour the royal icing green and pipe wiggly grass up the sides of the cake, as shown in the photograph below.

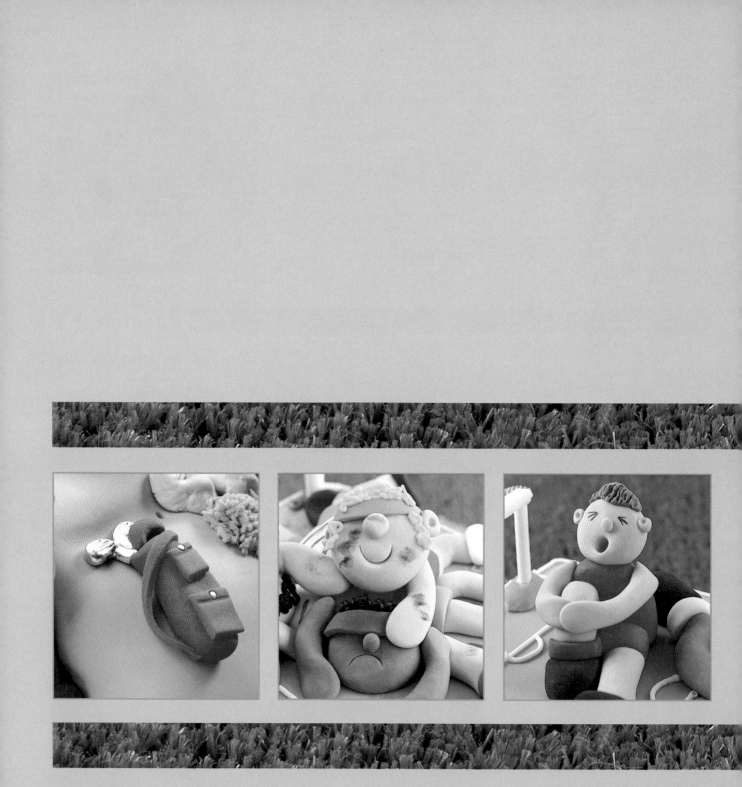

BALL SPORTS

GOLF

It is actually very easy to make standing-up figures out of sugarpaste, as long as there is something behind them that can provide support. In this case, it is the cake itself.

Cake and Decoration

20cm (8in) round sponge (layer) cake (see page 104)

1 quantity buttercream (see page 106)

Icing (confectioners') sugar for rolling out

Water for sticking sugarpaste (rolled fondant)

750g (1lb 10oz) green sugarpaste

20g (¾oz) brown sugarpaste

100g (3½oz) red sugarpaste

45g (1½oz) blue sugarpaste

30g (1oz) flesh-coloured sugarpaste (see page 106)

30g (1oz) white sugarpaste

30g (1oz) grey sugarpaste

1 strand raw dried spaghetti

Black food colour paste

Edible silver food colour (optional)

1 sheet rice paper

30g (1oz) soft brown sugar

Equipment

Carving knife

25cm (10in) round cake board

Rolling pin

Small sharp knife

Paintbrush

Wooden food skewer

Thin drinking straw

Scissors

Sieve

TIP
Make an edible golf club with gelatine or modelling icing.

1 Carve the cake into an irregular shape, making sure that there is an inlet where the golfer can stand and use the cake for support. Slice horizontally and fill with buttercream. Place on to the cake board and arrange some of the small cut-out pieces of cake around the sides and on the top of the cake. 'Glue' in place with buttercream, then spread a covering of buttercream all over the top and sides.

2 With a little water, moisten the visible areas of cake board around the sides and back of the cake. Dust a work surface with icing (confectioners') sugar and knead and roll out all the green sugarpaste (rolled fondant). Lift and place over the cake. Starting from the top of the cake to try to avoid air from getting trapped, smooth the icing into position, covering both the cake and the board. Trim and neaten the edges.

3 Remove a small piece of brown sugarpaste and set to one side. Divide the rest into

two equal parts and make into lozenge shapes for the golfer's shoes. Stick in position with a little water. To make the legs, roll about 50g (2oz) red sugarpaste into a chunky sausage and cut in half. Slice off and discard the two rounded outer ends of the sausages. Stick the legs on to the shoes and against the side of the cake. Remember to use the cake as support. The tops of the legs should be level to provide a platform on which to stand the body.

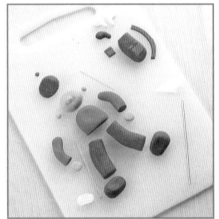

4 Roll about 30g (1oz) blue sugarpaste into a conical shape for the body. The top should be fairly flat, ready for the head. Stick the body on to the legs and against the cake. If you wish, you can stick a small section of dried spaghetti through the body for extra support.

5 Make a 15g (½oz) flesh-coloured ball for the head and a 10g (¼oz) red ball for the cap. Slice and discard about a third off each. Pinch and pull the front of the red ball to form a brim and stick on to the top of the head. Press a line into the

front of the cap with the back of a knife and make tiny cuts with the tip of a knife to suggest lines of stitching. Finish off with a tiny ball of blue.

6 Add a nose and two ears, then push the end of a paintbrush into each one to leave a slight hollow. Push the end of a wooden food skewer or paintbrush into the face to make the mouth.

7 Cut the wooden skewer down to size (about 8cm/3in). Position it so that it leans on the board and rests against the golfer's chest. (Remember to remove this when cutting the cake.) For arms, roll 10g (¼oz) blue sugarpaste into a sausage, cut in two and stick in place. Make two small flesh-coloured oval hands and stick on top of the golf club.

8 For the base of the club, make a small white sugarpaste lozenge shape and press a few lines down the length. Stick at the bottom of the club and then paint the handle black with food colour and the base of the stick with silver (if using).

9 To make the golf bag, use 30g (1oz) red sugarpaste. Pull off about 10g (¼oz) and roll the rest into a tapering sausage. Flatten slightly and slice a little off the thin end. Roll out the rest and cut out two tiny squares for pockets. Press a line with a knife and a circle with a drinking straw into each. Stick behind the golfer.

TIP
If the body or head start to lean, support them from behind with sugarpaste 'rocks'.

10 Make three upside-down 'L' shapes for the clubs out of white and brown. Press lines into the 'irons' with the back of a knife. Stick in place in the bag and paint silver if you wish. Pick out the buttons on the bag with silver dots. Cut a thin strip of red for the strap and drape and stick across the bag.

11 Partially knead together the grey and the rest of the white sugarpaste to make a marbled effect. Pull off little pieces and stick them around the cake to look like rocks. Push leftover green icing through a sieve to make bushes (see right) and use to hide any untidy areas on the cake. Place one largish rock towards the

rear in which to stand the flag. Make a slight hollow in front of it with the end of a paintbrush.

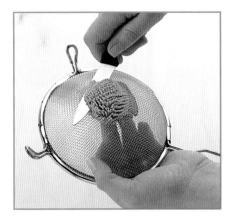

12 Cut a 10cm (4in) length of drinking straw and a triangle of rice paper. Make two holes in the rice paper and thread on to the straw. Stand in the rock behind the hole. Moisten the cake board and area around the golfer with a little water and spoon over the soft brown sugar to look like sand.

QUICK & EASY VERSION

A sitting character is always much quicker to make than a standing one. For this figure use the same shapes as for the main cake, but make her trousers shorter. Add a small sausage of pink sugarpaste on the end of each leg to give the impression that she is wearing knickerbockers.

TENNIS

By making the players on virtually any sporty cake look exhausted you add a touch of humour – and you save yourself the task of trying to get them to stand up!

1 For the net, make two gelatine or modelling icing posts or use two candy sticks (sweet cigarettes). Leave to dry.

2 Level the cake and turn upside down. Slice in half horizontally and sandwich with buttercream. Place diagonally on the cake board and cover with buttercream.

3 Dust a work surface with icing (confectioners') sugar and roll out and cover the cake using 1kg (2lb 4oz) white sugarpaste (rolled fondant). Smooth the top and sides, ideally using a cake smoother.

4 Neaten the base, then moisten the exposed cake board with a little water. Roll out and cover the board with four triangles cut out of 300g (10oz) green sugarpaste. Trim and neaten.

5 To make the court, paint a light line of water around the top of the cake about 2cm (¾in) from the edge. Dab a little in the centre too. Roll out 300g (10oz) green sugarpaste and lay on top of the cake.

Cut out a rectangle and peel away the excess. Place a little white royal icing into a piping bag fitted with a no. 2 piping tube (tip) and pipe the lines on to the court.

6 Push the posts into two green icing balls and stick either side of the court with royal icing. Measure the height and width between the centre of the two posts and cut a rectangle of net to that size. Pipe royal icing up the middle of each post and stick the net between.

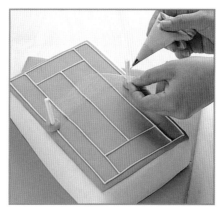

7 To make the lady, roll 10g (¼oz) white sugarpaste into a conical shape for her body (see page 53). Stick to the court. Roll and cut 10g (¼oz) of white into a rectangular shape for her skirt and press lines in it.

8 Roll 10g (¼oz) flesh-coloured sugarpaste into a sausage for legs and cut in half. Repeat, using 5g (⅙oz) flesh-coloured sugarpaste for her arms. Stick a 10g (¼oz) flesh-coloured ball between the arms for her head.

Cake and Decoration

1 quantity gelatine or modelling icing (optional) (see page 107) or 2 candy sticks (sweet cigarettes)

15 x 25cm (6 x 10in) sponge (layer) cake (see page 104)

2 quantities buttercream (see page 106)

Icing (confectioners') sugar for rolling out

Water for sticking sugarpaste (rolled fondant)

1 quantity royal icing (see page 108)

1.15kg (2lb 9oz) white sugarpaste

600g (1lb 4oz) green sugarpaste

75g (2½oz) flesh-coloured sugarpaste (see page 106)

20g (¾oz) brown sugarpaste

5g (⅙oz) yellow sugarpaste

1 strand raw dried spaghetti

Yellow, black and green food colour pastes

Equipment

Small sharp knife

Carving knife

30cm (12in) square cake board

Palette knife (metal spatula)

Cake smoothers (optional)

Fine and medium paintbrushes

5 piping bags (see page 107)

Nos. 1 and 2 piping tubes (tips)

Ruler or tape measure

Scissors

Net or tulle

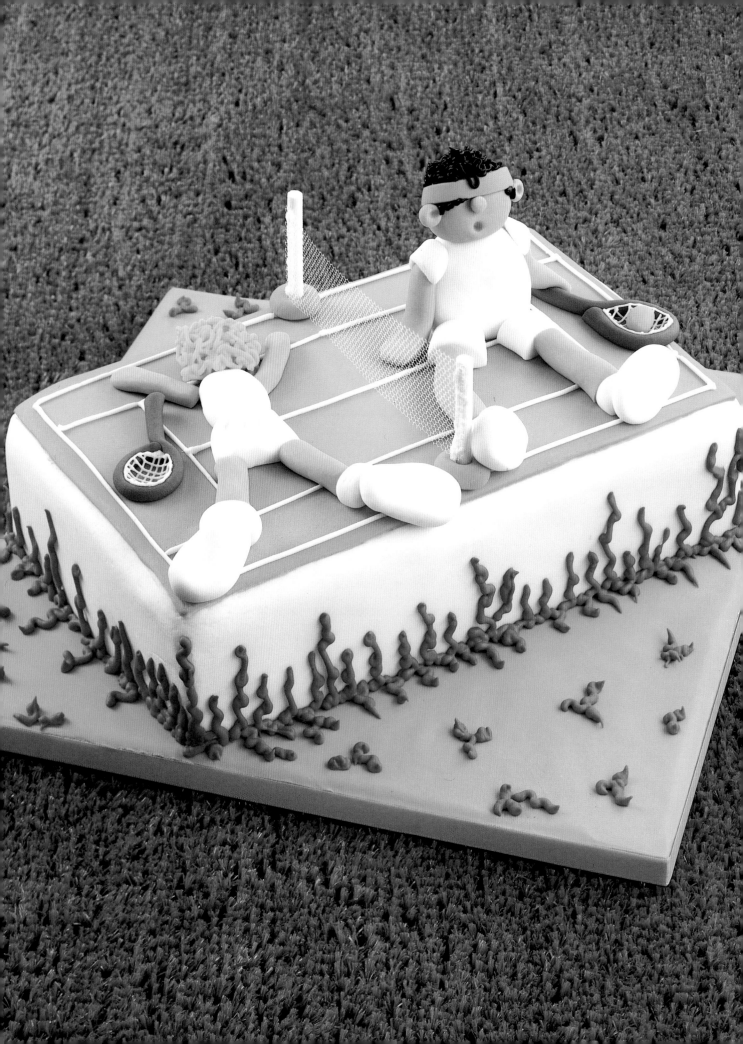

9 Make two white 5g (⅙oz) discs for socks and two white 10g (¼oz) ovals for shoes. Stick to her legs. Press a couple of lines in the socks with a knife. Place yellow-coloured royal icing or buttercream in a bag with a no. 1 piping tube (tip) and pipe wiggly hair.

10 To make the man, roll 45g (1½oz) white sugarpaste into a cone for his body. Stick this on the cake. Insert a length of spaghetti for extra support. Roll 10g (¼oz) white sugarpaste into a sausage for his shorts, cut in half and stick against his body.

11 Roll 20g (¾oz) flesh-coloured sugarpaste into a thinnish sausage for legs and cut in two. Stick to the cake. Add socks and shoes, as before. Roll 15g (½oz) flesh-coloured icing into a ball for the head, stick on his head and make a hollow for his mouth

with the end of a paintbrush. Stick a band of green around his head and add ears and a nose. Make a little hollow in each ear. Pipe hair using coloured royal icing.

12 To make two simple tennis rackets, roll out two 10g (¼oz) brown sugarpaste strings. Bend one end round in a circle and stick on top of the cake. Place a no. 1 piping tube into a piping bag, add royal icing and pipe strings across the racket (see above right).

13 Make two 5g (⅙oz) flesh-coloured sugarpaste arms and stick into place with one hand resting on the racket. Make sleeves by rolling 5g (⅙oz) white sugarpaste into a ball. Flatten and cut in half. Lay and stick a semicircle over each shoulder. Roll a little yellow sugarpaste into a ball and stick on one of the rackets.

14 Brush away any dusty icing sugar marks on the court with a damp paintbrush. (Any shiny streaky marks this causes will dry matt after a few hours.) Colour about 2 tablespoons royal icing or buttercream green and place in a piping bag fitted with a no. 2 piping tube. Pipe wiggly grass up the sides of the cake and a few clumps over the board.

QUICK & EASY VERSION
By simply altering the shape of the racket and colour and size of the ball, you can easily adapt a tennis player into virtually any other racket sport enthusiast. Because she is a lady, this player has a gentle glow about her. If, however, your version has a man on the top I would suggest painting big red cheeks on his face to increase the humour!

FOOTBALL

The scarf trick is a useful one to have up your sleeve when it comes to making any sporty cake. Not only does it emphasize the team you are supporting but it can also be used to hide any mistakes that may have happened while you were covering the sides!

Cake and Decoration

I quantity gelatine or modelling icing (see page 107)
15 x 25cm (6 x 10in) sponge (layer) cake (see page 104)
2 quantities buttercream (see page 106)
Icing (confectioners') sugar for rolling out
Water for sticking sugarpaste (rolled fondant)
1.3kg (2lb 14oz) green sugarpaste
350g (12oz) white or chosen colour sugarpaste
250g (9oz) red or chosen colour sugarpaste
75g (2½oz) brown sugarpaste
15g (½oz) blue sugarpaste
60g (2oz) black sugarpaste
90g (3oz) flesh-coloured sugarpaste (see page 106)
I quantity royal icing (see page 106)
Black food colour paste
I strand raw dried spaghetti

Equipment

Small sharp knife
Carving knife
30cm (12in) square cake board
Rolling pin
Cake smoothers (optional)
Fine and medium paintbrushes
Piping bag (see page 107)
No. 2 piping tube (tip)
Scissors
Net or tulle

Quick & Easy Version on page 59

1 For the goal posts, make ten gelatine or modelling icing sticks: six about 6cm (2½in) long and four 8cm (3in) long (there are extras here in case of breakages). Leave to dry overnight, turning once.

2 Level the cake and turn upside down. Slice in half horizontally once or twice and sandwich together with buttercream. Place diagonally on to the cake board and spread with buttercream.

3 Dust a surface with icing (confectioners') sugar, then roll out 1kg (2lb 4oz) green sugarpaste (rolled fondant) and cover the cake. Smooth the sugarpaste into position, then trim and neaten. Lightly moisten the exposed board and cover using four triangles cut out of 300g (10oz) green sugarpaste (see page 58).

4 To make the scarf, roll out 300g (10oz) white sugarpaste. Cut out two strips about 30cm (12in) long and slice one end of each into a fringe. Lay and stick against the sides of the cake so that they cross at the front. Paint food colour stripes on to the scarf or stick strips cut out of about 150g (5oz) red sugarpaste.

5 To assemble the goal posts, insert two of the shorter sticks into two 5g (⅛oz) balls of green sugarpaste and stick on the cake with royal icing 8cm (3in) apart. Use a piping bag and a no. 2 piping tube (tip) to pipe royal icing on each post and lay a longer stick over the top.

6 Cut netting to 8 x 9cm (3 x 3½in). Pipe one line of royal icing along the top of the goal and another along the back on the cake. Press one of the shorter edges of the net into the icing on the cake and bend and stick the opposite end along the top of the goal. Repeat with the second goal and pipe lines on the pitch.

7 To make the goalie, roll 20g (¾oz) white sugarpaste into an oval for his torso and stick sideways on the cake. Roll 10g (¼oz) brown sugarpaste into a ball for his head and stick on to the body. Make a hollow with the end of a paintbrush for his mouth. Make two 10g (¼oz) brown sausage shapes for his arms and flatten one end of each for hands. Stick above his head. Roll 15g (½oz) blue sugarpaste into a sausage for shorts and cut in half. Stick in place on the cake.

8 For legs, roll 30g (1oz) brown sugarpaste into a 6cm (2½in) long sausage and cut in half. Bend at the knees and stick in place. Make and stick two white 5g (⅛oz) discs for socks and two 10g (¼oz) black ovals for boots. Paint two black food colour dots for eyes and add a tiny brown nose. For the ball, use 15g (½oz) white sugarpaste and press a few lines with a knife. Stick behind the goalie.

9 Make a 30g (1oz) red cone for the cry baby's body and stick on the cake. Stick one 5g (⅙oz) red trouser leg in front.

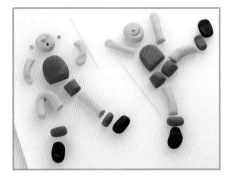

10 Roll 20g (¾oz) flesh-coloured sugarpaste into a sausage 12cm (5in) long. Cut in half and stick one leg flat on the cake. Bend the other in half and stick against the body. Make two red 5g (⅙oz) thick discs for socks and two 10g (¼oz) black ovals for boots. Stick in place. For extra support, stick a piece of spaghetti into the body. Roll 10g (¼oz) flesh-coloured sugarpaste into a ball for his head and stick in place.

11 Make a hole for the mouth and add two small flesh-coloured balls for ears and one for the cry baby's nose. Make small hollows for ears with the end of a paintbrush. Paint three lines for each eye and make hair from a short strip of brown sugarpaste. Press in lines with the back of a knife.

12 For arms, roll 10g (¼oz) flesh-coloured sugarpaste into a sausage. Cut in half and stick as though clasping his knee.

13 For the scorer's shorts, make 10g (¼oz) red sugarpaste into a rectangle, cut in half and stick level with the top of the cake. Use 15g (½oz) flesh-coloured sugarpaste to make a sausage for legs. Cut in half and stick on the cake side. Stick on two small red ovals and two larger black ones for socks and boots. Mould 30g (1oz) red sugarpaste into a cone for his body and 10g (¼oz) flesh-coloured sugarpaste for his head. Press in a smile, paint on eyes and add a nose. Make hair as before. For arms, roll 15g (½oz) flesh-coloured sugarpaste into a sausage and cut in half. Flatten the ends into hands and stick against his head.

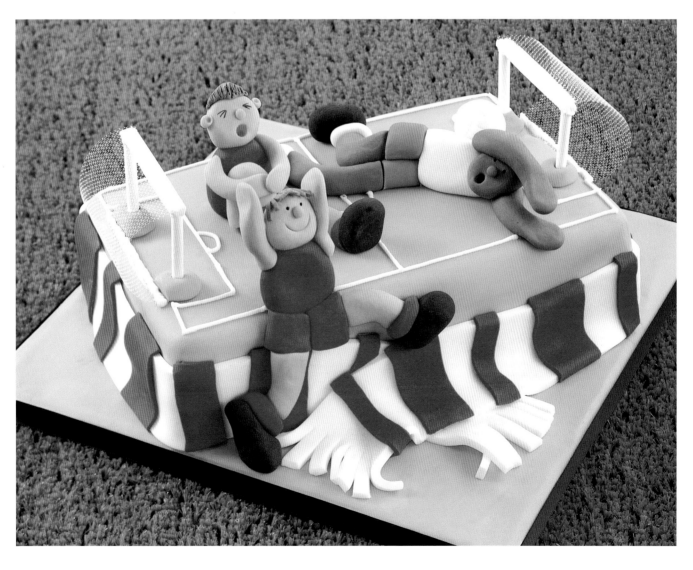

RUGBY

These rugby posts add an interesting three-dimensional aspect to the cake even though they are a little tiresome to make. However, do feel free to leave them out if you would rather – the recipient will still be able to recognize the theme of the cake!

Cake and Decoration

I quantity gelatine or modelling icing (optional) (see page 107)

I quantity royal icing (see page 106)

15 × 25cm (6 × 10in) sponge (layer) cake (see page 104)

2 quantities buttercream (see page 106)

Icing (confectioners') sugar for rolling out

Water for sticking sugarpaste (rolled fondant)

1kg (2lb 4oz) green sugarpaste

For players (this will alter depending upon the colour of your team's strips):

90g (3oz) red sugarpaste

250g (9oz) flesh-coloured sugarpaste (see page 106)

120g (4oz) white sugarpaste

100g (3½oz) brown sugarpaste

100g (3½oz) black sugarpaste

Yellow, green, black and brown food colour pastes

60g (2oz) green-coloured desiccated (shredded) coconut (see page 109)

Equipment

Small sharp knife

About 4 piping bags (see page 107)

Carving knife

30cm (12in) square cake board

Palette knife (metal spatula)

Rolling pin

Cake smoothers (optional)

Fine and medium paintbrushes

No. 2 piping tube (tip)

Quick & Easy Version on page 59

1 Make the goal posts from gelatine or modelling icing. Make six 15cm (6in) and four 10cm (4in) rods (to allow for breakages). Leave to dry for a minimum of 4 hours, turning at least once. Stick the posts together with royal icing and leave overnight.

2 Level the cake and turn upside down. Slice in half horizontally once or twice and fill the layers with buttercream. Reassemble and place on to the board. Spread a thin layer of buttercream, covering the top and sides.

3 Dust a work surface with icing (confectioners') sugar, knead and roll out 1kg (2lb 4oz) green sugarpaste (rolled fondant) and cover the cake. Smooth the icing and trim and neaten the base.

TIP
To help the coconut stay in place, smear the cake board with buttercream first.

4 For a rugby player, make a 45g (1½oz) red conical shape for a body. Add a 20g (¾oz) ball of flesh-coloured sugarpaste for a head. Make a hole with a paintbrush for a mouth or press the edge of a piping tube (tip) into the face for a smile or a frown. Stick a strip of sugarpaste across the head for a sweatband.

5 For arms, use 10g (¼oz) flesh-coloured sugarpaste rolled into a sausage shape. Flatten the end of each arm to make a hand and stick on the cake. For legs, make two 15g (½oz) flesh-coloured sausages and lay and stick flat on the cake or bend at the knee. Flatten 5g (⅛oz) white or coloured sugarpaste into a thickish disc for each sock and stick on each leg. Make a 10g (¼oz) black sugarpaste oval for each boot and stick one on to the end of each sock.

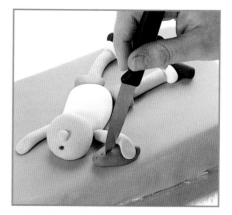

6 Roll 15g (½oz) brown sugarpaste into a rugby ball shape. Press a line of stitches along the top with the tip of a knife. Stick one of the player's arms over it.

7 Make three complete bodies and stack and stick them on top of each other. Fill any gaps with extra legs and arms. Pipe buttercream or royal icing hair or stick sugarpaste hair on your players if you prefer. Add noses, ears and eyes and any other details such as painted stripes on their strips. Daub the players with watered-down brown food colour to make them nice and muddy.

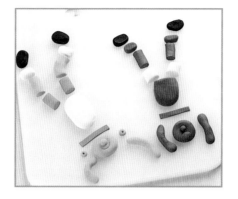

8 Place about 1 tablespoon white royal icing into a piping bag fitted with a no. 2 piping tube. Pipe a line around the edge of the cake (you can always leave this out if you wish).

9 Measure and make two hollows on each end of the cake with a wooden spoon handle, a goal post-width apart. Place about 1 tablespoon green-coloured royal icing into a piping bag fitted with

a no. 2 piping tube; alternatively, place the icing into the piping bag, fold to close and snip off a tiny triangle. Pipe the royal icing into the hollows and insert the goal posts. Pipe strands of grass around the base of each post. Spoon green-coloured coconut around the cake board.

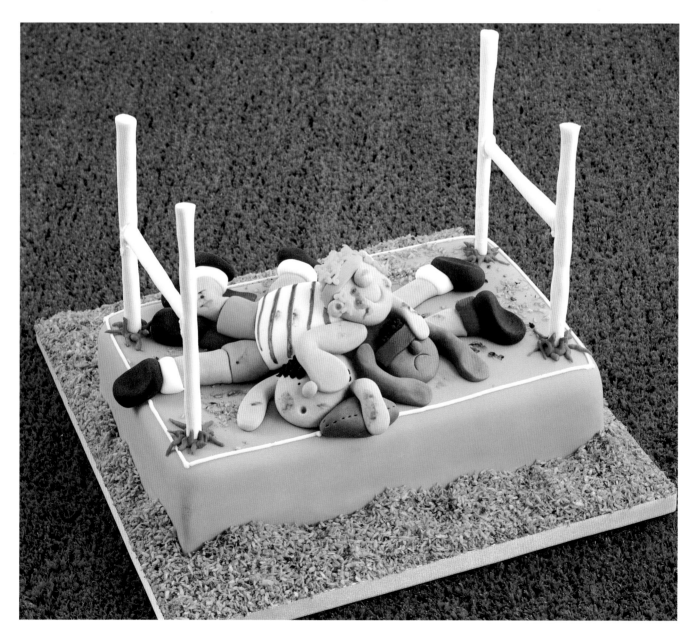

AMERICAN FOOTBALL

Although assembled in a similar way to the Rugby cake (see page 56), this cake still has its own identity. Dress the players in the recipient's favourite colours and leave out the posts if you run out of time.

Cake and Decoration

Gelatine or modelling icing (optional) (see page 107)

1 quantity royal icing (see page 106)

15 x 25cm (6 x 10in) sponge (layer) cake (see page 104)

2 quantities buttercream (see page 106)

Icing (confectioners') sugar for rolling out

Water for sticking sugarpaste (rolled fondant)

1.3kg (2lb 14oz) white sugarpaste

For players (this will alter depending upon the colour of your team's strips):

500g (1lb 2oz) red sugarpaste

250g (9oz) flesh-coloured sugarpaste (see page 106)

300g (10oz) blue sugarpaste

200g (7oz) yellow sugarpaste

250g (9oz) white sugarpaste

150g (5oz) brown sugarpaste

Black, brown and green food colour pastes

Equipment

Small sharp knife

4 piping bags (see page 107)

Carving knife

30cm (12in) square cake board

Palette knife (metal spatula)

Rolling pin

Cake smoothers (optional)

Fine and medium paintbrushes

No. 2 piping tube (tip)

Wooden spoon

1m (39in) ribbon

1 Make up at least two sets of goal posts as for the Rugby cake on page 56.

2 Prepare and buttercream the cake in the same way as well (see page 56) and place diagonally on the cake board. Dust a work surface with icing (confectioners') sugar and roll out and cover the cake using 1kg (2lb 4oz) white sugarpaste (rolled fondant). Smooth the top and sides and trim and neaten the base.

3 Moisten the cake board around the cake with a little water. Roll out 300g (10oz) white sugarpaste and cover the exposed cake board with four flat triangles. Trim and neaten the edges.

4 For each player, use 100g (3½oz) red sugarpaste for the torso. Shape the sugarpaste into a sort of upside-down triangular shape and stick on to the cake.

5 For the top of the legs, roll 15g (½oz) white sugarpaste into a sausage shape and cut in

half. Roll 10g (¼oz) red sugarpaste into a smaller sausage and cut in half to make the lower legs. Stick all the leg sections in place, bending them at the knees if you wish.

6 Stick two 10g (¼oz) white oval shapes on the end of each leg for boots. Make a 20g (¾oz) red ball for his helmet (again the colour will depend on your team's colours) and two 15g (½oz) sausage shapes for his arms. Stick into position. Flatten two 5g (⅙oz) balls of flesh-coloured sugarpaste to make the hands and stick on the ends of his arms. Stick a flat oval of flesh-coloured sugarpaste on the front of the helmet and a small white or coloured oval just below that for the chin protector.

7 Make three players one at a time and pile them on top of each other, as for the Rugby cake. Then add extra legs, arms and heads to give the impression of there being more players than there really are. Make a small brown lemon shape for the ball and place under one of the arms.

TIP
If you hate piping, stick thin sugarpaste strings on the helmet instead.

8 Place 1 tablespoon white royal icing into a piping bag fitted with a no. 2 piping tube (tip) and pipe the masks on to each face. Pipe around the face first then across and down twice. Pipe numbers on to the players' backs. Stick a small flesh-coloured sugarpaste nose on to each of the player's faces and paint two dots for eyes.

QUICK & EASY VERSIONS

Each of these cakes demonstrates a neat cake-decorating trick, which would work with any sport. By arranging the figure so he appears to be bursting out of the top of the cake, you avoid having to make legs! Just make a body and head, and stick them in the centre of the cake. Add arms and arrange them in whatever position you wish – they could even be holding a ball or a bat. Then add the facial features and hair. To finish, paint some jagged cracks around the base of the player using black food paste and a fine paintbrush.

9 Paint a little watered-down brown and green food colour around the cake to make the pitch look muddy, and erect the goal posts as on the Rugby cake.

10 Pipe grass around the base of the posts. Wrap a ribbon around the side of the cake, sticking the join with royal icing.

TRACK AND FIELD

ATHLETICS

Dress the athletes in whatever colours you like. To add an Olympic flavour, you could paint the Olympic rings on the top or add a candle to represent the Olympic flame.

Cake and Decoration

20cm (8in) round sponge (layer) cake (see page 104)

1 quantity buttercream (see page 106)

Icing (confectioners') sugar for rolling out

Water for sticking sugarpaste (rolled fondant)

750g (1lb 10oz) white sugarpaste

200g (7oz) chestnut-coloured sugarpaste

blue, green, black and red food colour pastes

1 quantity royal icing (see page 106)

6 candy sticks (sweet cigarettes), see Tip page 65

15g (½oz) light brown sugar

For each athlete

Shoes: 5–15g (⅛–½oz) black/white sugarpaste

Socks: 5g (⅛oz) coloured sugarpaste

Legs: 10–20g (¼–¾oz) flesh-coloured sugarpaste (see page 106)

Shorts: 5g (⅛oz) coloured sugarpaste

Body: 10–20g (¼–¾oz) coloured sugarpaste

Head: 10g (¼oz) flesh-coloured sugarpaste

Arms: 10–20g (¼–¾oz) flesh-coloured sugarpaste

Equipment

30cm (12in) round cake board

Carving knife

Rolling pin

Cake smoothers (optional)

Fine and medium paintbrushes

At least 2 piping bags (see page 107)

No. 2 piping tube (tip) (optional)

Wooden food skewer or raw dried spaghetti

1 Level the cake and turn upside down. Slice in half horizontally and fill with buttercream. Place in the centre of the cake board and spread buttercream around the sides and top.

2 Dust a work surface with icing (confectioners') sugar, then knead and roll out 750g (1lb 10oz) white sugarpaste (rolled fondant). Check that the buttercream is still tacky. If it has hardened, spread another quick covering over the first layer to provide a good adhesive for sticking the sugarpaste to the cake. Place the sugarpaste over the cake. Smooth and trim away any excess around the base.

3 Moisten the cake board with a little water. Knead and roll 175g (6oz) chestnut-coloured sugarpaste into a long, thin strip about 92cm (36in) long. Cut a little off one long side and roll up the icing like a loose bandage. Placing the neat edge of the strip up against the cake, then unwind the icing around the cake to cover the board. Trim and neaten the join and edges.

4 Re-knead and roll out all the remaining chestnut-coloured sugarpaste and cut out a rectangle measuring about 18 x 8cm (7 x 3in). Stick this on top of the cake to form the long jump. Roll out about 15g (½oz) white sugarpaste and cut out four thin strips. Lay and stick these in a rectangle on top of the chestnut-coloured sugarpaste to form a frame in which to place the sand.

5 Using a little watered-down blue food colour, paint simple curves for clouds around the sides of the cake.

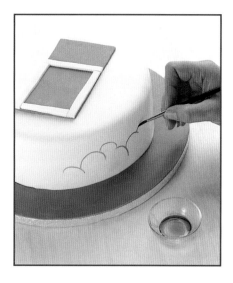

6 Place 3 tablespoons green royal icing into a piping bag. Fold over the end a couple of times to close and snip a tiny triangle off the end. Pipe wiggly lines up the cake sides to look like grass. Cut the end off a second piping bag and insert the piping tube (tip). Put in 1 tablespoon white royal icing and pipe lines around the board to denote the running track and a couple across the run-up on the long jump. Alternatively, press lines into the icing with a knife.

> **TIP**
> **When making the athletes themselves, the secret is to use the sides of the cake to provide support. Always begin with the feet and work up.**

7 To make each runner, stick one oval shoe (about 10g/¼oz black or white sugarpaste) on the board next to the cake and a second about half way up the cake. Stick a small ball of blue or white sugarpaste on top of each for socks and press a few lines into them with the back of a knife. Next, make two 10g (¼oz) flesh-coloured sugarpaste sausages for his legs. Slice a little off each end and bend both at the knee and stick on to the cake.

8 To make the shorts, roll out about 5g (⅙oz) of whatever colour sugarpaste you like. Cut out two small rectangles and stick on top of the legs. Next, roll about 15g (½oz) of sugarpaste in your team's colours into a cone and stick on top of the shorts, pressing securely against the side of the cake. The top should be slightly flat so that it can support the head. Then roll about 10g (¼oz) of

flesh-coloured sugarpaste into a ball for the head and stick into position. For extra security you can insert a strand of raw dried spaghetti into the runner's body and slot the head on top.

9 Add hair either by piping some coloured royal icing in a wiggly pattern or you could use a strip or fringe of coloured sugarpaste instead. Paint features on the face with black food colour and add a tiny sugarpaste nose and ears. Make a small hollow in each ear with the end of a paintbrush and one for a mouth if you want to give your athlete an anguished expression. If your athlete has dark skin, you might find it better to stick two tiny white sugarpaste dots on to the face for his eyes and then paint on the pupils. Add a splodge of red food colour on the cheeks of each athlete to give a flushed look!

10 To make the arms, roll about 10g (¼oz) flesh-coloured sugarpaste into a sausage and cut in half. Stick the arms in whatever position you wish. I turned my runners into a relay team by giving one of them a small strip of black sugarpaste to hold as a baton.

11 The hurdler was made in exactly the same way as the runners except with a hairband and pony tail. These were made by

sticking a tiny flattened ball and a tapering sausage of sugarpaste on the top of her head. Paint a couple of stripes on her top and running shoes with black food colour. The hurdles themselves are simply candy sticks (sweet cigarettes) glued into position with royal icing.

12 For the long jumper, make two small ovals for the feet and place in the sandpit on top of the cake. Roll about 10g (¼oz) flesh-coloured sugarpaste into a sausage and cut in half for his legs. Bend each in half and stick upright in the sandpit next to, but not touching, the feet. Roll about 15g (½oz) sugarpaste into a cone for the body and sit in the pit. Add head, hair, features and arms as for the runners. Carefully spoon the light brown sugar into the sandpit. With a paintbrush, splodge a little watered-down green food colour around the top of the cake to look like grass.

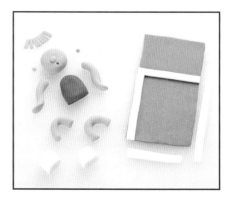

TIP
You can also use gelatine or modelling icing to make the hurdles. You will need three small sticks for each hurdle (see page 107).

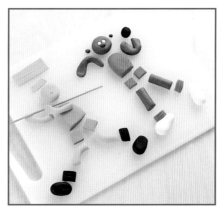

13 The body of the javelin thrower is made in the same way as for the runners except that both her feet are on the ground next to the cake. The javelin itself is a wooden food skewer cut to length (about 20cm/8in), stuck behind the athlete's head and held in place by the arms. If you prefer, make a gelatine or modelling icing one (see page 107) or use a strand of raw dried spaghetti – but don't forget to remove it before you cut the cake.

14 For the shot putter, use the same body design as for the runners but have both feet resting on the ground. Make a small ball of black sugarpaste for the shot. Rest one arm casually on the cake and bend the other one in half so that it can hold the shot where it is tucked beneath the athlete's chin.

QUICK & EASY VERSION

To make a sitting athlete, begin with the shorts. Roll about 15g (½oz) sugarpaste into a sausage and bend into a semicircle. Slice a little off both ends to neaten them and stick towards the rear of the cake. Roll 15–30g (½–1oz) sugarpaste, depending on how chunky you want your athlete to be, into a cone and stick on top of the shorts. If you wish, you can stick a strand of raw dried spaghetti through the torso for extra security. Stick a small semicircle of flesh-coloured sugarpaste over the top of the body to turn his top into a vest. Add head, arms, legs, socks and boots, as shown in the main cake. Dab watered-down green food colour around the top of the cake to look like grass.

TRAINERS

This design could be used for virtually anyone in almost any sport. It would also make a good cake for a teenager. Don't be put off by having to carve the cake into a shape. It is easier than you think and, if you go wrong, you can glue mistakes with buttercream. Nobody will see them under the sugarpaste.

Cake and Decoration

18cm (7in) square sponge (layer) cake (see page 104)

1 quantity buttercream (see page 106)

Icing (confectioners') sugar for rolling out

Water for sticking sugarpaste (rolled fondant)

1.3kg (2lb 14oz) white sugarpaste

100g (3½oz) blue sugarpaste

100g (3½oz) green sugarpaste

60g (2oz) black sugarpaste

90g (3oz) brown sugarpaste

1 tablespoon white royal icing (optional) (see page 106)

Equipment

Carving knife

30cm (12in) round cake board

Rolling pin

Small sharp knife

Veining and bone tools (optional)

Paintbrush

Piping bag (see page 107)

No. 4 piping tube (tip) (optional)

Scissors

1 To carve the cake, first cut away the square corners to make them softly rounded. Next, cut a V-shaped groove down the centre and continue down the middle, from front to back to give the effect of a pair of shoes. Carefully finish the shaping by slightly rounding the bottom edges of the trainers.

2 Slice the cake horizontally and sandwich with buttercream. Reassemble and place on to the centre of the cake board. Spread more buttercream all over the top and sides of the cake.

3 Roll 90g (3oz) white sugarpaste (rolled fondant) into a sausage measuring about 23cm (9in) long. Lay it in a doughnut shape on one of the ankles (see above right). Repeat on the second trainer and then moisten both doughnuts with a little water.

4 Dust a work surface with icing (confectioners') sugar and knead 1kg (2lb 4oz) white sugarpaste until pliable. Roll it out and lift and lay over the cake. Starting with the ankles, gently press the icing into position. (It does not matter if it tears in the centre of the ankle as this will be hidden later.)

5 Gently press the icing into the groove between the trainers and over the top and sides. Trim and neaten the base. Using either a veining tool or the back of a knife, press two lines down the front of each trainer, so that they meet in a point just above the toe.

> **TIP**
> **To personalize the cake, copy the design of your sportsman's favourite trainers.**

6 Using either a bone tool or the end of a paintbrush, push pairs of five lace holes into the front of each trainer. Try not to go through into the cake beneath.

7 Thinly roll out the blue sugarpaste and cut out triangular and rectangular shapes for each trainer. Stick in place with a little water. Repeat, using the green. Roll out the black sugarpaste and cut out two black discs. Stick one in the centre of each ankle. Re-roll the leftover black icing and cut out two wide semicircular shapes. Stick one on the front of each toe.

8 Moisten the exposed cake board around the cake with a little water. Carefully knead together 120g (4oz) white sugarpaste and 90g (3oz) brown to make a woodgrain effect (see Aerobics cake on page 91). Roll out the sugarpaste and cover the board around the trainers in four strips. Carefully ease it into awkward areas such as between the trainers. Trim and neaten the edges around the board.

9 Place about 1 tablespoon of white royal icing or buttercream in a piping bag fitted with a no. 4 piping tube (tip).

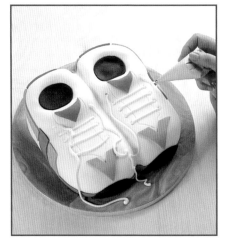

Alternatively, place the icing straight into the bag, close and snip a tiny triangle off the end. Pipe laces across the front of each trainer and falling on to the covered board.

10 Dust away any icing sugar smudges on the cake or board with a soft damp paintbrush.

TIPS
If you hate piping, roll out some thin sugarpaste laces instead.
Leave the board plain if you prefer.

QUICK & EASY VERSION

This version demonstrates how easily you can convert the trainer design into football boots. Make sugarpaste ovals and press a hollow into one end with a bone tool or the end of a wooden spoon. Press a few lines in the front of the boot with the back of a knife and paint a design in black food colour. Paint some green food colour on the cake and position the boots. Pipe royal icing or buttercream laces. You may also be able to find small tubes of ready-made writing icing in the supermarket, which are ideal for tasks such as these. The design is painted on the ball but if you find this too fiddly, copy the easy football used on the Football cake on page 54 instead.

ROLLERBLADING

Decorating Variation

Make this cake variation using a 20cm (8in) square cake and a 30cm (12in) square cake board. Carve a simple boot shape out of the cake (template provided on page 110).

To achieve the height difference in the heel, first cut a rounded curve into the bottom right-hand corner of the boot, but do not let your knife go right through the cake.

Slice through the cake horizontally and the heel section should automatically

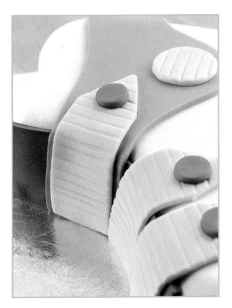

come away. Slice and fill the cake with buttercream, reassemble and then coat the top and sides. Cover using 1.3kg (2lb 14oz) sugarpaste.

To make identical-sized wheels, either use a circle cutter or a lid as a cutter. Alternatively, roll and squash four same-sized sugarpaste balls.

Finally, cut out three rectangles and a disc from yellow sugarpaste. Cut the

rectangles into points, then stick over the front of the boot. For the ribbed effect on the straps, roll out the sugarpaste and then lightly press lines into it with a ruler. Finish off with three flattened discs of blue.

To change this design into an ice skating boot, leave off the wheels and stick a thin strip of grey sugarpaste along the base to look like a blade.

SHOW JUMPING

How could any horse refuse to leap such a delicious looking jump? If you cannot obtain any candy canes because they are out of season do not despair, simply substitute drinking straws instead or make a hedge jump out of the bushes shown in the Golf cake on page 48.

Cake and Decoration

5 candy canes

1 quantity royal icing (see page 106)

20cm (8in) square sponge (layer) cake (see page 104)

1 quantity buttercream (see page 106)

Icing (confectioners') sugar for rolling out

Water for sticking sugarpaste (rolled fondant)

1kg (2lb 4oz) white sugarpaste

120g (4oz) green sugarpaste

250g (9oz) grey sugarpaste

70g (2½oz) dark brown sugarpaste

60g (2oz) black sugarpaste

30g (1oz) pale brown sugarpaste

30g (1oz) flesh-coloured sugarpaste (see page 106)

Black and green food colour pastes

Equipment

25cm (10in) square cake board

Rolling pin

Cake smoothers (optional)

Small sharp knife

Carving knife

Fine and medium paintbrushes

2 piping bags (see page 107)

Star piping tube (tip) (optional)

Scissors

1 To make the jump, cut the candy canes into three 12cm (5in) lengths, two 5cm (2in) lengths and two 1.5cm (½in) chunks. Stick them together with dabs of royal icing and leave to dry as long as possible, preferably overnight.

2 Level the top of the cake and turn upside down. Slice and sandwich the cake with buttercream and place off-centre on the cake board. Buttercream around the sides and top of the cake.

3 Dust a work surface with icing (confectioners') sugar and knead and roll out all the white sugarpaste (rolled fondant) to a width of about 36cm (14in). Place over the cake and smooth into position. Trim and keep any off-cuts from around the base.

4 Lightly moisten the exposed cake board around the base of the cake with a little water. Knead and roll out the green sugar-

paste and cut into four thin strips. Lay these over the cake board so that they overlap. Make a diagonal cut from each corner of the cake board to the corresponding corner of the cake, then lift and remove the excess icing to leave a neat join. Trim and neaten the edges all around the board.

5 To make the horse's body, roll 100g (3½oz) grey sugarpaste into a cone. Stick on top of the cake with water. The widest part should be about 1cm (½in) in from the edge of the cake. Roll 60g (2oz) grey into a sausage shape for the head. Pinch a slight 'waist' into the middle of the sausage to make a nose and lay and stick against the body. With the end of a paintbrush, make three holes for nostrils and a mouth.

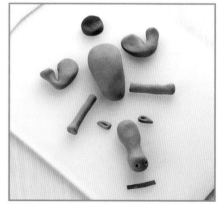

6 Stick two little triangles on top of the head for the ears and press a line into each one with the end of a paintbrush. Make two tapering 10g (¼oz) sausages for the

front legs and stick either side of the head. Make two 20g (¾oz) sausage shapes for the rear legs about 6cm (2½in) long. Bend each in half. Flatten one end slightly to form the hoof and press and stick the other end against the body to form the thigh.

7 Roll 5g (⅛oz) dark brown sugarpaste into a lozenge shape for a saddle and stick on the horse's back. Tweak one end up slightly. Stick a thin strip of brown across the horse's nose.

8 Start with the rider's feet. Make two 15g (½oz) black sugarpaste sausages and mould into 'L' shapes with flat tops. Stick on the board and against the side of the cake. Roll 30g (1oz) pale brown sugarpaste into a sausage about 10cm (4in) long. Slice a little off each end and stick in a curve between the two boots. Press and stick against the cake's side.

QUICK & EASY VERSION

Make the horse's head, then stick an almost flat brown ball next to it for the rider's body. Follow the instructions for the main cake for decorating the horse and rider's heads, but position the rider's arms as though hugging the horse instead of pushing it.

9 Roll 45g (1½oz) dark brown sugarpaste into a cone for the rider's body and stick in position. Roll 15g (½oz) dark brown sugarpaste into a sausage and cut in two for the arms. Bend each in half and stick from the rider's shoulder to the rear of the horse. Make and position two flesh-coloured ovals for hands.

> ### TIP
> ### *For extra security, slot a strand of raw dried spaghetti through the head and body.*

10 For the head, roll 20g (¾oz) flesh-coloured sugarpaste into a ball and stick on to the body. Cut out a thin brown rectangle for the hair. Press lines down its length with the back of a knife and lay over the top of the head. Paint the features on the face with black food colour and add a few checks on the jacket and arms.

11 Make and stick three flesh-coloured balls on the head for ears and a nose. Poke a hollow in each ear with the end of a paintbrush. Roll 10g (¼oz) black sugarpaste into a ball for the rider's helmet. Slice a little off the base and pinch and pull the front forwards to form a brim. Press a line across the front of the helmet with a back of a knife. Stick on to the head.

12 Colour about 3 tablespoons royal icing green and place in a piping bag. Snip a tiny triangle off the end and pipe wiggly lines up the sides of the cake to look like grass. For the horse's mane, colour 2 tablespoons

royal icing grey and either fill a bag fitted with a star tube (tip) or do as you did for the grass. Pipe squiggly lines over the horse's face and neck. Pipe a line on to each hoof and brush with a damp paintbrush to give a hairy effect.

13 Partially knead together any leftover white, black and grey sugarpaste to make a marbled effect. Pull off little pieces and roll into 'rocks'. Stick the jump in position with royal icing. Support it with rocks and pipe grass up the sides to hide any messy bits. Finally, dab a little watered-down green food colour over the top of the cake.

MOTOR RACING

Once you have assembled this cake, you will not only have learnt how to put a race track together, but you will also know how to make a cake in the shape of the figure eight – should you ever need to make one!

1 Level the tops of both cakes and turn upside down. Slice a little off one side of both cakes so that they can be pushed together. Slice and fill with buttercream and place diagonally on the cake board. Cover the top and sides of the cakes with a layer of buttercream.

2 To make the undulating countryside, divide and roll 150g (5oz) white sugarpaste (rolled fondant) into various-sized balls and lay against the sides of the cake. Moisten the exposed cake board and the sugarpaste balls with a little water.

3 Dust a work surface with icing (confectioners') sugar and knead all the green sugarpaste. Roll it out to about 36cm (14in) in diameter and lift and place over both the cake and the board.

4 Carefully smooth the icing into position and trim and neaten the edges of the board. Keep the leftover icing. Do not worry if

you get any cracks or tears in the icing. You can hide these with bushes and rocks later.

5 Carefully paint a light line of water around the top of the cake about 1.5cm (½in) in from the edge. Ensure you do not drip water in the centre!

6 Roll out all the grey sugarpaste and lay on top of the cake. Using the tip of a sharp knife, cut through the grey sugarpaste about 1cm (⅛in) in from the edge. Remove the excess. Cut a figure eight shape out of the centre of the grey and remove that too. Keep the leftover grey for making rocks later.

7 To make the bodies of the cars, roll 30g (1oz) each of the pink, yellow, red and blue sugarpastes into chunky carrot shapes (see overleaf). Slice a little off the rounded ends and cut the sliced pieces into rectangles. Stick one of these on the back of each of the cars.

Cake and Decoration

2 x 15cm (6in) round sponge (layer) cakes (see page 104)

1 quantity buttercream (see page 106)

Icing (confectioners') sugar for rolling out

Water for sticking sugarpaste (rolled fondant)

200g (7oz) white sugarpaste

1.5kg (3lb 6oz) green sugarpaste

200g (7oz) grey sugarpaste

45g (1½oz) pink sugarpaste

45g (1½oz) yellow sugarpaste

30g (1oz) red sugarpaste

30g (1oz) blue sugarpaste

50g (1¾oz) black sugarpaste

Black food colour paste

Equipment

Carving knife

30cm (12in) square cake board

Rolling pin

Cake smoothers (optional)

Small sharp knife

Jumbo drinking straw

Fine and medium paintbrushes

Piping tube (tip) or small round lid

Sieve

8 Roll 5g (⅙oz) white or black sugarpaste into a ball for each helmet and stick one on the top of each car. Knead together the leftover pink and yellow sugarpaste to make a flesh colour. Roll out and cut out four tiny rectangles. Stick one on each helmet.

9 Holding the drinking straw at a slight angle, press a smile on to the faces of three of the drivers. The fourth car has careered off the track so make a dismayed expression for the driver's mouth with the end of a paintbrush.

10 Thinly roll out 10g (¼oz) white sugarpaste and cut out four small discs using a piping tube (tip) or something similar as a cutter. Stick one on the front of each car. With black food colour, paint a number on each car, and dots for the drivers' eyes.

11 Roll the remaining black sugarpaste into a sausage. Slice it up to make the wheels. Stick four around each car and place the others in piles around the track.

TIP
You could paint the recipient's age on one of the cars.

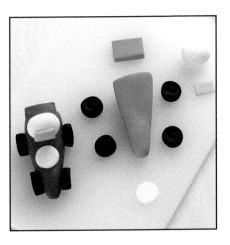

Press a circle into each wheel with the end of the drinking straw. Stick the cars into position on the cake. Paint a couple of watery black lines behind the crashed car to look like skid marks.

12 To make the rocks, lightly knead together the leftover white and grey sugarpastes until a marbled effect is obtained (see Fishing cake on page 82). Pull off little

chunks and roll into differently shaped and sized small pebbles. Stick them all around the cake.

13 To make the bushes, push the leftover green sugarpaste through a sieve (see Golf cake on page 48). Stick around the cake, hiding any problem areas.

14 Dust away any icing sugar smudges with a damp paintbrush. Any wet, shiny areas will revert to a matt finish within a couple of hours.

QUICK & EASY VERSION

Cover the top of the cake with a round of green sugarpaste and a wavy grey 'track'. Alternatively, you could just dab on some green food colour. The cars are made in exactly the same way as before, and the cake is finished off with a few sugarpaste bushes made by pushing green sugarpaste through a sieve. If you know that you are going to be short of time nearer the occasion, you can make the cars a couple of weeks in advance. Keep them in a box until needed.

MOTORBIKE RACING

Quite often you will get people asking to keep the little models on a cake. On this design, the model is actually on its own thin cake board on top of the cake. This means it can be easily removed all in one piece.

Cake and Decoration

1 quantity gelatine or modelling icing (see page 107)

Candy sticks (sweet cigarettes) (optional)

Icing (confectioners') sugar for rolling out

20cm (8in) round sponge (layer) cake (see page 104)

1 quantity buttercream (see page 106)

Water for sticking sugarpaste (rolled fondant)

2 tablespoons royal icing (see page 106)

850g (1lb 12oz) white sugarpaste

50g (1¾oz) black sugarpaste

60g (2oz) red sugarpaste

5g (⅙oz) flesh-coloured sugarpaste (see page 106)

Red, black and gooseberry green food colour pastes

Edible silver food colouring (optional)

Equipment

Rolling pin

Circle cutters or small lids

Template for engine (see page 110)

Small sharp knife

Carving knife

25cm (10in) round cake board

15cm (6in) round thin cake board

Cake smoothers (optional)

3 plastic cake dowels (see Step 5)

Paintbrushes (fine and medium)

Piping bag (see page 107)

No. 3 piping tube (tip)

1m (39in) ribbon

1 Make the gelatine or modelling icing first. Dust a work surface with icing (confectioners') sugar and roll out about 45g (1½oz) gelatine icing. Cut out a wheel about 5cm (2in) in diameter and about 1.5cm (½in) thick. A cutter or small lid is the easiest way to do this. Press a smaller circle in the centre and leave to dry. Make two.

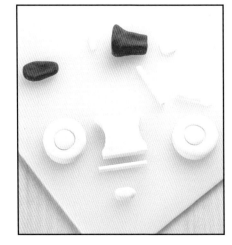

2 Roll out some more gelatine icing to the same thickness as the wheels and cut around the bike centre template. Leave to dry. Make two thin stick shapes for the exhaust and the handlebars, and a third for the front spoke. Squash one end of the spoke to make it into a spoon shape. Leave to dry overnight, turning over at least once.

3 Level the top of the sponge (layer) cake and turn upside down. Slice horizontally into two or three layers and sandwich together with buttercream. Place in the centre of the cake board and spread a thin covering of buttercream over the top and sides.

4 Dust a work surface with icing sugar and roll out 700g (1lb 12oz) white sugarpaste (rolled fondant) and cover the cake with it. Smooth the top and sides and trim and neaten around the base.

5 The plastic cake dowels are used to stop the weight of the bike from squashing the cake and squeezing buttercream out of the sides. Use as shown on the Cricket cake on page 35. (You will not need them if you are using a fruit cake.)

6 Lightly moisten the cake board around the cake. Roll out 100g (3½oz) white sugarpaste and cut out a strip about 60cm (24in) long. Roll up the icing loosely like a bandage and unwind and lay around the base of the cake. Trim and neaten the edges of the board.

7 Moisten the small board with water and cover using 60g (2oz) white sugarpaste. Trim and neaten the edges. Stick the wheels and middle section of the bike upright on the board with royal icing.

> **TIP**
> *Candy sticks, or sweet cigarettes as they used to be called, make ideal ready-made exhaust pipes and handlebars.*

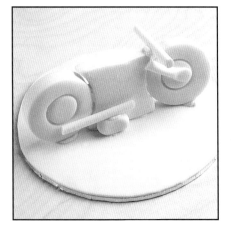

QUICK & EASY VERSION

This cake would be suitable for anyone interested in any sport that involves wearing a crash helmet. Make the helmet out of a red sugarpaste disc. Stick a smaller flesh-coloured one on top and paint eyes, shoulders and a zip with black food colour. The nose is a ball of flesh-coloured sugarpaste and the glove began as an oval. Make a cut for the thumb and curl back the rest of the finger area into the palm of the hand to produce a 'thumbs-up' greeting.

8 Stick the spoke on to the front wheel and the exhaust against the back one. Support the exhaust from below with a small blob of sugarpaste. If you think you would find it easier, you can paint the wheels, exhaust and so on, now, before the rider is put in position.

9 Roll 45g (1½oz) black sugarpaste into a sausage about 20cm (8in) long for the biker's legs. Bend both ends to form feet and lay and stick the legs over the centre of the bike. The knees should be bent and the feet flat on the floor to provide extra stability for the bike.

10 To make the fairing for the bike, roll 30g (1oz) red sugarpaste into a pointed conical shape. Slice a little of the pointed end ready for the headlight and pinch and pull around the other end to fan it out slightly. Stick the fairing on top of the front wheel.

11 For the back of the bike, roll 10g (¼oz) red sugarpaste into an oval shape. Stick it behind the biker's legs and tweak the end upwards slightly.

12 Roll 30g (1oz) white sugarpaste into a cone for the rider's body. Stick it on the bike, leaning forward slightly. For the arms, roll 10g (¼oz) white sugarpaste into a sausage about 6cm (2½in) long. Cut in half, bend both at the elbows and stick against the rider's body.

13 For the motorbiker's hands, stick two small black discs on his wrists and over the handlebars (see above right). Roll a little white sugarpaste into a ball and squash to form a disc for the headlight. Stick on to the front of the motorbike and make a criss-cross pattern with the back of a knife.

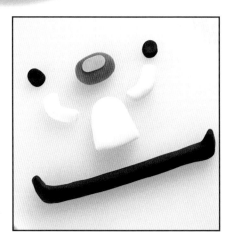

14 Roll 15g (½oz) red sugarpaste into an oval for the rider's head and stick on to the body. Stick a flat, flesh-coloured oval on the front of the helmet and a flat, white disc on the front of the bike.

15 Using food colour, paint eyes on the rider, red and black stripes on his jacket, and a number on the bike. Paint the tyres black and the wheel centres, spoke and exhaust silver or grey.

 16 Dab some green food colour around the base of the motorbike. Knead together any leftover white and black sugarpaste to make rocks and stick these around the motorbike. You can use the rocks to provide extra support if your bike is a little wobbly.

17 Place the bike in position on top of the cake and pipe around the edge of the board with a little white royal icing. Use a technique called a 'snail trail'. Squeeze a little icing out of the piping tube (tip), release the pressure in your fingers and pull slightly. Squeeze and release again all the way around. Alternatively, just pipe dots or leave plain. Lay the ribbon around the base of the cake. Trim to fit and secure with royal icing.

CYCLING

Decorating Variation

If you are ever asked to make a bicycle of any sorts, this really is the easiest way to do it – lie it on the ground! The other secret is not to over complicate it. Bikes are full of cogs and wheels and all sorts of other spindly bits that would be a nightmare to copy individually, so try to simplify it to the most basic components. This lets the viewer's eye read 'bike', but you won't be driven insane making it. Use a 15cm (6in) square sponge (layer) cake and a 20cm (8in) square cake board. The spokes are painted on to the top of the cake with a little black food colour.

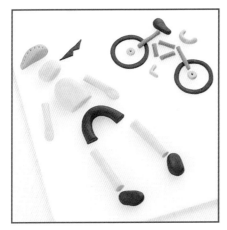

SOLO SPORTS

FISHING

Apparently, fishing is one of the most popular sports in the world. So with all those eager fishermen after them, I felt it was only right that in this case the fish should be the one with the upper hand – or should I say fin!

Cake and Decoration

1 sponge (layer) cake baked in a pudding bowl (see page 105)
1 quantity buttercream (see page 106)
Icing (confectioners') sugar for rolling out
Water for sticking sugarpaste (rolled fondant)
450g (1lb) white sugarpaste
150g (5oz) grey sugarpaste
30g (1oz) black sugarpaste
60g (2oz) light green sugarpaste
90g (3oz) blue sugarpaste
75g (2½oz) flesh-coloured sugarpaste (see page 106)
90g (3oz) dark green sugarpaste
10g (¼oz) orange sugarpaste
2 strands raw dried spaghetti
Black, ice blue, mint green and dark brown food colour pastes
3 tablespoons royal icing (optional) (see page 106)

Equipment

25cm (10in) round cake board
Carving knife
Fine and medium paintbrushes
Rolling pin
Small sharp knife
Drinking straw
2 wooden food skewers, cut to 12cm (5in) lengths, or 2 sticks made from gelatine or modelling icing (see page 107)
2 x 50cm (20in) lengths thread
Palette knife (metal spatula)

1 Turn the cake upside down and place towards the rear of the cake board. Cut it horizontally once or twice and fill with buttercream. Reassemble and spread more buttercream all around the outside of the cake.

2 To give the cake its irregular shape, divide and roll about 120g (4oz) white sugarpaste (rolled fondant) into various sized balls and stick them around and on the cake itself. Moisten the sugarpaste balls with a little water.

3 To achieve the marbled rock effect, partially knead together 150g (5oz) grey and 300g (10oz) white sugarpaste. Dust a work surface with icing (confectioners') sugar, roll out the icing and lift and place over the top of the cake. Smooth it into position and trim and neaten the base. Roll any leftovers into small pebbles and arrange around the cake base.

4 To make the first fisherman, roll 30g (1oz) black sugarpaste into a sausage shape and cut in half. Tweak each half into 'L' shapes for his boots. Stick into position against the cake. Roll 30g (1oz) light green sugarpaste into a sausage shape for his legs. Cut in half and stick on top of the boots and against the cake. Roll 30g (1oz) blue sugarpaste into a conical shape for his body and stick on top of the legs.

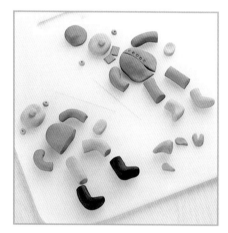

5 Make two 10g (¼oz) blue sausage shapes for his arms. Bend each one at the elbow and press and stick on to the body. Stick a short length of raw dried spaghetti into his body to provide extra support and slot on a 20g (¾oz) flesh-coloured oval for his head. Stick two small balls either side of the head for ears and one on his face for his nose. Make a hollow in each ear with the end of a paintbrush. See Quick & Easy Version for hair.

6 For the second fisherman, make light green boots and blue trouser legs in exactly the same way as you did for the first and stick them on to the cake. Roll 45g (1½oz) dark green sugarpaste into a conical shape for his coat. Pinch and

pull the front of the coat to fan it out slightly and cut a split in the middle. Press a line down the centre and press tiny circles with the tip of a drinking straw to look like buttons.

7 To make the collar, thinly roll out about 5g (⅙oz) dark green sugarpaste and cut out a rectangle. Make a partial cut halfway across the middle of the rectangle and splay to form a collar. Stick on top of his coat and insert a length of spaghetti into the body for extra support.

8 Roll 20g (¾oz) dark green sugarpaste into a sausage and cut in half for his arms. Stick these on to his body. Make a head out of a 20g (¾oz) ball of flesh-coloured sugarpaste and stick on top of the body. Add ears and a nose, as before.

9 Squash 10g (¼oz) dark green sugarpaste into a disc for the cap. Pinch and pull the front forwards slightly to form a peak and stick on top of his head. Paint features on both characters with black food colour and a fine paintbrush.

10 Tie a length of thread to one end of each skewer. Press one against each fisherman and hold in place with a 5g (⅙oz) flesh-coloured sugarpaste oval.

11 To make the water, place 3 tablespoons of buttercream or royal icing into a bowl. Add

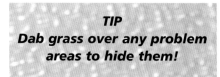

a little ice blue and mint green food colour paste and partially mix into the icing. Use a small palette knife (metal spatula) to smear the icing around the cake. You can use a paintbrush to push it into awkward areas or lift some rocks if you find it easier.

12 Make the fish's head by rolling about 5g (⅙oz) orange sugarpaste into a cone. Bend the head forwards slightly and stick into the water. Make a small disc for his tail. Cut a tiny nick in the centre and pull it apart to splay slightly. Stick this in the water behind the head.

13 Paint the face on the fish with black food colour paste and also add a few scales. Those

angry eyebrows are not hard to do, they are simply a couple of 'S' shapes. Carefully tie together the ends of the fishing lines to make a bow and hook under the fish's head. Make two tiny orange fins and stick on to the side of the fish as though holding the line.

14 Spatter a little green buttercream or royal icing on top of the rock to look like lichen or grass.

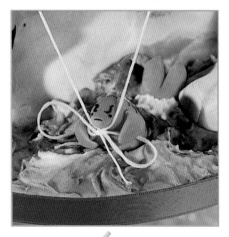

QUICK & EASY VERSION

For a windswept look, mix a little brown food colour into either royal icing or buttercream and pat on to the top of the character's head with the flat of a knife. The fisherman consists of a sugarpaste body only, and he has a green rectangle with a small square cut out stuck on his front to give the impression that he is wearing waders. Instead of a fish, this time he has caught a nice tasty boot.

SNOOKER

The dramatic floor tiles give this cake a strikingly masculine look. Feel free to leave them all one colour for a softer finish or if you don't feel up to all that painting. And before anyone writes in to correct me, I know that snooker balls don't normally sit on the floor, but it looked good artistically!

1 Begin by covering the cake board. Lightly dampen it all over with a little water and cover with 300g (10oz) white sugarpaste (rolled fondant). Use the all-in-one covering method shown in the Armchair Supporter cake on page 88. Trim and neaten the edges of the cake board and make a tiled impression by pressing lines at right angles to each other with a clean ruler. Place the covered board to one side.

2 Level the top of the cake and cut a 5cm (2in) strip off one side. Place the strip against the smaller side of the remaining cake and trim to make a rectangle measuring about 10 x 20cm (4 x 8in). Slice the cake in half horizontally and fill with a layer of buttercream. Reassemble the cake and spread a thin covering of buttercream over the top and sides.

3 Roll out 300g (10oz) black sugarpaste and cut out a long strip that measures about

60 x 8cm (24 x 3in). Slide a knife underneath the strip to make sure it is not stuck to the work surface and roll up like a bandage. Unwrap around the sides of the cake. If necessary, trim the top edge level with the top of the cake.

4 To cover the top of the cake, roll out 200g (7oz) green sugarpaste and lay on top of the cake. Trim to fit. Don't worry about getting perfectly straight, neat edges as they will be hidden by the sides of the table. Carefully lift the cake and place it diagonally on the covered board.

5 To make the table legs, roll out 120g (4oz) brown sugarpaste to a thickness of about 5mm (¼in) and cut out four rectangles about 4cm (1½in) wide. Wrap and stick one around each corner and trim level with the top of the table (see overleaf). Paint a line of water around the top edge of the table and roll 150g (5oz) brown sugarpaste

Cake and Decoration

15cm (6in) square sponge (layer) cake (see page 104)

½ quantity buttercream (see page 106)

Icing (confectioners') sugar for rolling out

Water for sticking sugarpaste (rolled fondant)

300g (10oz) white sugarpaste

300g (10oz) black sugarpaste

200g (7oz) green sugarpaste

325g (11oz) brown sugarpaste

75g (2½oz) blue sugarpaste

90g (3oz) red sugarpaste

30g (1oz) flesh-coloured sugarpaste (see page 106)

5g (⅙oz) pale green sugarpaste

5g (⅙oz) yellow sugarpaste

5g (⅙oz) pink sugarpaste

1 strand raw dried spaghetti

Black food colour paste

Equipment

25cm (10in) square cake board

Fine and medium paintbrushes

Rolling pin

Small sharp knife

Clean ruler

2 wooden food skewers, cut to about 18cm (7in) lengths (optional) (See Quick & Easy Version on page 87 for edible alternatives)

Ball tool (optional)

into a sausage about 60cm (24in) long. Flatten slightly with a rolling pin and, starting at the top left-hand corner, lay and stick in position. Using the end of a paintbrush or a ball tool, gently press six small hollows into the green 'baize' around the edge of the table to represent the pockets.

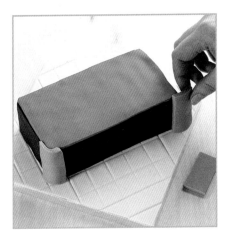

6 Make the player's feet first. Divide 30g (1oz) brown sugarpaste in half and roll into two ovals. Slightly squash one end of each shoe and stick one on the floor next to the table and the other at an angle just behind it. Remove 5g (⅙oz) from the blue sugarpaste and put to one side. Roll the rest into a sausage about 18cm (7in) long for his legs and cut in half. Starting with the back leg, stick one end on the shoe and bend slightly at the knee. Stick and press the leg against the side of the cake so that it stands level with the top of the cake. Repeat with the front leg. If necessary, trim the top of the leg to the same height as the table.

7 Roll 30g (1oz) red sugarpaste into a chunky triangular shape for the player's body. Stick it on top of the trousers and table edge. It should bend forwards slightly. Insert a short length of spaghetti for extra support if you wish. For his arms, roll 20g (¾oz) red sugarpaste into a sausage and cut in half. Bend both the arms at the elbow and stick on the sides of the player's body.

8 Make two small flesh-coloured ball shapes for his hands. Place one of the food skewers in position and stick the hands in place to hold it securely. Roll 20g (¾oz) flesh-coloured sugarpaste into a ball for his head and stick on to the body. Make a small hollow for his mouth with the end of a paintbrush. To make his hair, roll out about 20g (¾oz) brown sugarpaste and press lines into it with the back of a knife. Cut out a semicircle and a leaf shape. Stick the semicircle over the back of his head and the leaf shape over his forehead for a quiff.

9 Stick three small flesh-coloured balls on to his face: two for his ears and the third for a nose. Press a shallow hollow into each ear with the end of a paintbrush. Paint two black food colour dots for his eyes, and also paint alternate squares on the floor in black food colour to give it a chequered effect.

10 While the floor is drying, make the snooker balls. Make about six red and one each of green, yellow, pink, black, blue and white. Position on the table in suitable places. Make a tiny blue square for the chalk and press a little hollow in the top with the end of a paintbrush. Stick on the edge of the table.

11 To make the ball holder, roll out about 5g (⅙oz) brown sugarpaste and cut out a thin strip and form into a triangle. Stick the triangle and a couple of balls on the floor. Finally, rest the second skewer (the cue) on the table so that it hides the join in the edge of the table.

QUICK & EASY VERSION

This is simply a circle of green sugarpaste on top of the cake with the triangle, various balls and two wooden food skewer cues arranged on the top. Paint the handles of the cues with black food colour to make them look more authentic. If using skewers worries you, make the cues from gelatine or modelling icing (see page 107) or lie sugarpaste cues on the top of the cake instead. You could also use dried spaghetti.

ARMCHAIR SUPPORTER

We all know one. Someone who sits glued to the television, endlessly speculating on how they could do better, how the referee doesn't know anything, how they would run the team if they were the manager, and so on.

Cake and Decoration

25cm (10in) square sponge (layer) cake (see page 104)

1 quantity buttercream (see page 106)

Water for sticking sugarpaste (rolled fondant)

Icing (confectioners') sugar for rolling out

300g (10oz) mixture of any coloured sugarpastes for the carpet

750g (1lb 8oz) purple sugarpaste (see page 108)

140g (4½oz) black sugarpaste

375g (12oz) white sugarpaste

90g (3oz) brown sugarpaste

150g (5oz) flesh-coloured sugarpaste (see page 106)

90g (3oz) blue sugarpaste

45g (1½oz) green sugarpaste

15g (½oz) grey sugarpaste

1 strand raw dried spaghetti

Black and blue food colour pastes

Equipment

30cm (12in) square cake board

Carving knife

Rolling pin

Small sharp knife

Fish slice (optional)

Cake smoothers (optional)

Fine and medium paintbrushes

Bone tool (optional)

Piping tube (tip) or small lid

1 Moisten the cake board with a little water and lightly knead together a 300g (10oz) mixture of any coloured sugarpaste (rolled fondant). Do not over knead or it will turn a muddy brown. Dust a work surface with icing (confectioners') sugar and roll out to about 15cm (6in) wide. Lift the sugarpaste and place it on the board. Continue to roll up to and over the edges of the board. Neaten the edges and place the board to one side.

2 Slice the cake as shown above right. The two largest sections form the base and back of the armchair and the two thin strips make the arms. The remaining two pieces will be used for the television and table that stand near the armchair.

3 Place the chair back and arms into position on top of the base. If necessary, trim to fit and slightly round the edges of the back. Stick everything into place with buttercream. You can also slice and fill the base horizontally with a layer of

buttercream. Cut the remaining two small pieces of cake into rectangles for the television and the table, making the television smaller than the table. Spread buttercream over the outside of all three cakes.

4 Knead and roll out all the purple sugarpaste to a thickness of about 5mm (¼in). Lift and place over the chair cake. Smooth the icing into position and trim. You might find it easier if you cut a small cross into the seat area (see Swimming cake on page 22). This will stop air from getting trapped. The figure and cushions will hide the exposed cake later.

5 If you have a fish slice, slide it under the back of the cake and carefully lift and place into position on the cake board. If you don't, then use the flats of your hands or a couple of cake smoothers to lift the cake without denting the sides. Poke a spotty pattern all over the chair using the end of a paintbrush, trying not to go through into the sponge beneath.

6 Roll out the leftover purple sugarpaste (you should have about 200g/7oz) and cut out a long, thickish strip about 60 × 4cm (24 × 1½in) for the frill. Run a knife under the length of the strip to make sure it is not stuck to the work surface and press

lines along one edge using the end of a paintbrush. Paint a line of water around the base of the chair and roll up the strip like a loose bandage. Starting from the back, unwind the frill and stick it around the chair. Using the end of a paintbrush make a line of small dents along the top of the strip and a line of stitching using the tip of a sharp knife.

7 To make the television and table, cover the larger of the remaining sections of cake with 90g (3oz) brown sugarpaste and the smaller with 60g (2oz) black. Trim and neaten around the bases and dab a little buttercream on top of the table. Place the television on top. Roll out about 20g (¾oz) white sugarpaste and cut out a small rectangle for the television screen. Stick in place and paint a simple picture on the screen using food colour (see pages 108–9).

8 Knead together about 60g (2oz) white and 30g (1oz) purple sugarpaste to make a pale mauve. Roll out and cut into two

squares for the cushions. Tweak the ends into points and stick on to the back of the chair.

9 Thinly roll out 60g (2oz) white sugarpaste and cut out a rectangle for the rug. Press lines across the width of the rug with the back of a knife and fringe both ends. Lay and stick in an irregular manner on the floor.

10 For the supporter's boots, make two 30g (1oz) black ovals. Stick one in front of the chair and the other at the side at an angle. Make two thick 15g (½oz) white disc shapes for socks and press lines across them so they look as though they are all scrunched up. Stick on top of the boots.

QUICK & EASY VERSION

Make the television set out of a square of black sugarpaste. Alter the sport shown if you wish or write a birthday wish to the recipient. Instead of sitting, the figure lounges across the top of the cake, which means he does not need any internal supports such as spaghetti to hold him in place. Personalize him/her by changing the hair colour or outfit to look like the recipient.

11 Roll 60g (2oz) flesh-coloured sugarpaste into a sausage for the legs and cut in half. Lay and stick the legs from the top of the socks to the seat of the chair, letting one drape over the arm of the chair. Roll 45g (1½oz) white sugarpaste into a sausage for his shorts. Slice off the two rounded ends and bend into a 'U' shape. Stick in the seat of the chair.

12 Roll 90g (3oz) blue sugarpaste into a conical shape for his torso. Slice a little off the base (keep for making the arms later) and stick the body on top of the shorts. Take 30g (1oz) flesh-coloured

sugarpaste and set a tiny quantity aside. Roll the rest into a head and stick on top of the body. Using either a bone tool or the end of a paintbrush, make a hole in the lower part of his face and pull downwards slightly to give him an outraged expression. Stick the leftover flesh-coloured sugarpaste in the centre of his face for his nose.

13 Next, roll out about 30g (1oz) white sugarpaste and cut out a strip for his scarf. Cut a fringe in one end of the strip and lay and stick it down the front of his body. Scrunch up and re-roll the leftover icing and cut out a shorter white strip. Stick this around the top of his body. Roll the leftover blue sugarpaste into an oval shape and cut in half to make the two sleeves. Stick to the body.

14 Roll 60g (2oz) flesh-coloured sugarpaste into a sausage about 17cm (7in) long and cut in half for the arms. Slightly flatten the rounded end of each half to make hands and stick into position.

15 Place the table and television in position on the board. Stick a 5g (½oz) ball of black on top of the television and insert two short strands of spaghetti. Paint them black using food colour paste and stick two tiny black sugarpaste dots on the top.

16 Thinly roll out about 90g (3oz) white sugarpaste and cut out two long strips for scarves. Fringe both ends of each scarf and drape and stick one over the television set and the other on the floor.

17 To make the beer cans, roll 45g (1½oz) green sugarpaste into a sausage and cut into three. Roll out about 15g (½oz) grey sugarpaste and, using a piping tube (tip) or small lid as a cutter, cut out six small discs. Stick the discs on either end of each green section and paint a tiny black triangle on one end. Stick the cans in place. Finally, paint the stripes on the scarf with blue food-colour paste and brush away any icing (confectioners') sugar marks with a damp paintbrush.

AEROBICS

This cake should strike a chord with anyone who has ever puffed their way through a step or aerobics lesson. At least at this particular class, there is no 'going for the burn' – unless you had a bit of a disaster at the baking stage, that is! On this design, all the hairstyles are created in buttercream, but substitute sugarpaste if you prefer.

1 Slice any excess sponge cake off the top of the cake to level it, then turn it upside down so that the widest part forms the base. Slice it two or three times horizontally and reassemble, sandwiching the layers with buttercream. Place the cake diagonally on the cake board and spread buttercream all over.

2 Dust a work surface with icing (confectioners') sugar and roll out 350g (12oz) purple sugarpaste (rolled fondant). Cut out a 60 x 4cm (24 x 1½in) strip. Slide a palette knife (metal spatula) under it to loosen it from the surface and gently roll up the strip like a loose bandage. Starting from the back, lay it around the bottom edge of the back.

3 Repeat with 200g (7oz) pink sugarpaste, cutting it into a 4.5cm (1¾in) wide strip. Stick around the cake on top of the purple. Finally, roll out about 175g (5½oz) turquoise sugarpaste and lay on top of the cake. Trim to fit on top of the pink.

4 Next, make some woodgrain-effect sugarpaste for the floor. Use about 90g (3oz) brown sugarpaste and 150g (5oz) white. Roll the two colours together to make a sausage, then fold in half. Re-roll and fold again. Continue for 8–10 times until you see a woodgrain effect appearing. Moisten the cake board around the cake with water.

5 Roll out the sugarpaste and cover the board with four sugarpaste triangles. Smooth it into position and trim and neaten the edges. Using a knife, press lines into the floor to resemble floorboards.

6 For the instructor's feet, make two 20g (¾oz) black sugarpaste ovals. Stick one oval on the floor and the other oval halfway up the aerobics step. Make two 5g (⅛oz) ovals for socks and press lines into each one with the back of a knife. Stick them on to the instructor's feet.

Cake and Decoration

Sponge (layer) cake baked in 1kg (2lb) loaf tin (pan) (see page 105)

1 quantity buttercream (see page 106)

Icing (confectioners') sugar for rolling out

Water for sticking sugarpaste (rolled fondant)

425g (15oz) purple sugarpaste

250g (9oz) pink sugarpaste

175g (5½oz) turquoise sugarpaste (see page 106)

90g (3oz) dark brown sugarpaste

200g (7oz) white sugarpaste

65g (2½oz) black sugarpaste

200g (7oz) flesh-coloured sugarpaste (see page 106)

60g (2oz) blue sugarpaste

Equipment

Carving knife

Palette knife (metal spatula)

25cm (10in) square cake board

Rolling pin

Cake smoothers (optional)

Small sharp knife

Fine and medium paintbrushes

2 piping bags (see page 107)

Scissors

7 Make two 10g (¼oz) flesh-coloured sausages for his legs. Bend each one at the knee and stick on to the socks and against the side of the cake. Make his unitard out of a 45g (1½oz) blue sugarpaste cone. Make a cut in the base, splay slightly and stick on to the legs and against the cake. Stick a short length of spaghetti into his body to give support. You can also place some leftover sugarpaste behind him if necessary.

QUICK & EASY VERSION

Just putting one exhausted pupil on the cake should raise a laugh and a knowing nod from the recipient! The lady here is made in exactly the same way as for the main cake. Make the towel on the floor out of a small sugarpaste rectangle. Press lines across its width with the back of a knife and fringe the two ends. Stick the towel on to the cake.

8 Cut out a tiny flesh-coloured sugarpaste semicircle and stick on the top of his unitard. Roll 15g (½oz) flesh-coloured sugarpaste into a ball for his head and roll and cut a 10g (¼oz) sausage in half for his arms. Stick on a tiny ball of sugarpaste for his nose. Dab chocolate buttercream on top of his head. Paint black food colour eyes, mouth and line for the microphone wire. Stick a tiny ball of black sugarpaste on the end of the wire.

9 For the sitting lady's feet, make two 10g (¼oz) white sugarpaste ovals and stick on the side of the cake. Make two 5g (⅙oz) white ovals for her socks. Press lines in as before and stick on to her feet. For the body, roll 30g (1oz) pink sugarpaste into an oval and stick on top of the cake. Roll 30g (1oz) flesh-coloured sugarpaste into a sausage for her legs. Cut in half, slice off the rounded ends and stick on the cake.

10 Make a 10g (¼oz) flesh-coloured ball of sugarpaste for her head and stick on the body.

Make a hollow with the paintbrush for her mouth and stick a strip of pink sugarpaste across her head. Stick on a tiny ball of sugarpaste for a nose. Make and cut in half a 20g (¾oz) sausage of flesh-coloured sugarpaste for her arms. Put a tablespoon of buttercream into a piping bag. Fold over the end twice, snip a tiny triangle off the pointed end and pipe squiggles for hair.

11 To make the collapsed pupil, roll 60g (2oz) purple sugarpaste into an oval and stick on the step. Make a thick, flattish round disc for her head using 15g (½oz)

flesh-coloured sugarpaste and make a hollow for the mouth. Stick in position. Roll 15g (½oz) sugarpaste into a sausage and cut in half for her arms. Stick one hanging off the step's edge, the other over her face. Roll 20g (¾oz) sugarpaste into a sausage for her legs and cut in half. Stick in place and add feet made from 5g (⅙oz) white ovals. Pipe chocolate buttercream hair.

12 The pupil peeping behind the step consists of only a head and hands. Make two 5g (⅙oz) ovals for her hands and stick on the top of the step. Make a head as for the first lady but this time lay the sweatband slightly higher on the head, paint in some eyes and add a couple of tiny balls for ears. Make a couple of dumbbells by rolling leftover sugarpaste into tiny sausage shapes. Squeeze the centres slightly to make an authentic dumbbell shape. Finally, dab a little red food colour on each of the pupils' cheeks to give them a puffed-out look. But avoid the instructor's cheeks – for some annoying reason, they never do more than glow slightly, do they!

JUDO

It is really worth stocking up with ribbon for your cakes around Christmas time as all sorts of exciting designs flood on to the market, which you can use throughout the year ahead. Don't despair if you cannot find anything similar to the ones I have used, as plain ribbon will work just as well for this cake, but always use a wide width – not only will it cover any cracks or problems with your sugarpaste covering, it will also save you having to pipe a design around the base.

Cake and Decoration

20cm (8in) square sponge (layer) cake (see page 104)

1 quantity buttercream (see page 106)

Icing (confectioners') sugar for rolling out

Water for sticking sugarpaste (rolled fondant)

1.4kg (3lb 1oz) white sugarpaste

200g (7oz) black sugarpaste

20g (¾oz) yellow sugarpaste

120g (4oz) flesh-coloured sugarpaste (see page 106)

45g (1½oz) brown sugarpaste

Black food colour paste

Equipment

Carving knife

20cm (8in) square cake board

Rolling pin

Cake smoothers (optional)

Small sharp knife

Fine and medium paintbrushes

90cm (36in) ribbon

Scissors

Adhesive tape

1 Level the top of the cake and turn it upside down. Slice horizontally and fill with buttercream. Reassemble and place in the centre of the cake board. Spread a thin covering of buttercream over the top and sides. Dust a work surface with icing (confectioners') sugar and knead and roll out 1kg (2lb 4oz) white sugarpaste (rolled fondant) to a thickness of about 5mm (¼in). Lift and place over the cake. Smooth all over, trimming excess from the base.

2 To make the mat, knead and roll out 200g (7oz) black sugarpaste. Dab a little water on the top of the cake itself and place the black on top. Cut a square into the black and peel away the excess. Don't worry about doing anything about icing sugar marks at this stage. They will get far worse before getting better!

3 Knead 5g (⅛oz) yellow sugarpaste into 300g (10oz) white to form a light cream colour for the judo suits. Begin with the male player on the floor. Roll 75g (2½oz) cream sugarpaste into a sausage about 18cm (7in) long. Cut in half to form the legs and stick on to the mat.

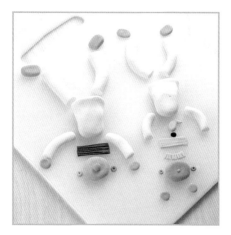

4 Roll 45g (1½oz) cream sugarpaste into a conical shape for the body and pinch along the base to thin it. Lay it on the mat with the thinned edge overlapping the tops of the legs slightly. Roll 15g (½oz) cream sugarpaste into a sausage, about 8cm (3in) long, and cut in half for the arms. Lay and stick to the body.

5 Make a 30g (1oz) flesh-coloured sugarpaste ball for the head, two 10g (¼oz) oval shapes for the feet and two 5g (⅛oz)

disc shapes for the hands. Stick in the appropriate positions. Roll out 5g (⅛oz) brown sugarpaste and press lines down its length for the hair. Cut out a rectangle and drape and stick over the top of the head. Stick a small ball of flesh-coloured sugarpaste on to the front of the face for a nose and one on each side of the head for the ears. Poke a slight hollow into each ear with the end of a paintbrush. Roll out about 5g (⅛oz) of the leftover black sugarpaste and cut out a thin strip for his belt. Drape and stick over his waist.

6 For the second figure, again begin with the legs. Roll 60g (2oz) cream-coloured sugarpaste into a sausage about 15cm (6in) long. Cut in half and bend each leg at the knees. Stick into position, one on the mat next to the first character's left leg, the other on top of both legs. Roll 45g (1½oz) cream sugarpaste into a conical shape for the body. Thin the base, as before, and stick into position on top of the first character.

QUICK & EASY VERSION

You could put any of the characters from the Judo or Wrestling cakes in a sitting position on top of this cake. But you can also turn the character into a boxer simply by adding boxing gloves. Make two red balls for the gloves and two tiny ovals for the thumbs.

7 Roll 15g (½oz) cream-coloured sugarpaste into a sausage for the arms and halve. Stick in position. Make a 20g (¾oz) flesh-coloured ball for the head, two small balls for hands and two 5g (⅛oz) ovals for feet, then stick in place. Thinly roll 15g (½oz) yellow sugarpaste and press lines down the length. Cut out a rectangle and stick to the head. Cut out a tiny rectangle, fringe along one edge and stick to the forehead.

8 Stick a small ball of black on the girl's head and a thin strip across her waist for her belt. Scrunch up the leftover yellow and form into a tapering sausage shape for the pony tail. Press lines down the length and stick on to the black ball. Add a tiny dot of flesh-coloured sugarpaste for the nose and two slightly larger ball shapes for ears. Press a hollow into each one with the end of a paintbrush. Paint in the eyes and mouth with a little black food colour.

9 To make the wood-effect flooring around the base of the cake, use 75g (2½oz) white sugarpaste and 30g (1oz) brown (see Aerobics cake on page 91).

TIP
Leave the cake board plain or cover with one-colour sugarpaste if you prefer.

10 Moisten the cake board around the base of the cake and roll out the wood-effect sugarpaste. Cover the board in four sections as shown on the Show Jumping cake on page 70.

11 Finally, place the ribbon around the base of the cake. Stick one end on top of the other at the back of the cake with a little adhesive tape. Dust away any icing sugar smudges on the black mat with a damp paintbrush and leave to dry.

WRESTLING

Decorating Variation

The wrestling characters lie in exactly the same positions as the judo players; it is just their outfits and expressions that are different. Make them as for the main cake.

The poles around the wrestling ring are plastic cake dowels (available from cake decorating shops). Buy two and cut them in half by scoring lightly with a serrated knife, then bend and snap them in half. Insert into the four corners of the cake, leaving at least 5cm (2in) protruding from the top.

Wind some silver embroidery thread around the poles to make the 'ropes' and top each pole with a small flattened ball of black sugarpaste. Remove the 'wrestling ring' before slicing and serving.

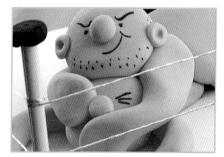

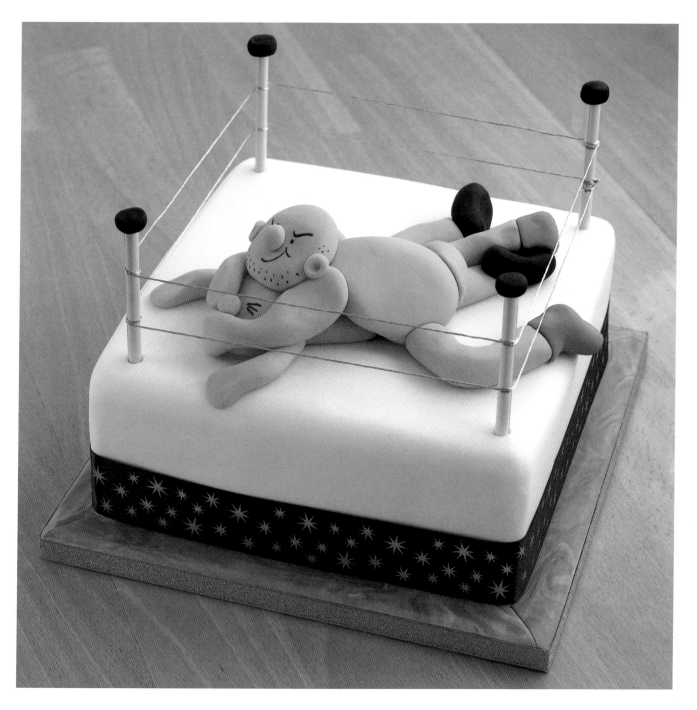

BUNGY JUMPING

Here is a real action cake for people who like excitement both in their spare time and in their icing!

Cake and Decoration

Gelatine or modelling icing (see page 107)

Assorted food colour pastes including blue, brown and black

18cm (7in) square sponge (layer) cake (see page 104)

1 quantity buttercream (see page 106)

Icing (confectioners') sugar for rolling out

Water for sticking sugarpaste (rolled fondant)

150g (5oz) grey sugarpaste

700g (1½lb) white sugarpaste

100g (3½oz) dark green sugarpaste

100g (3½oz) light green sugarpaste

1 quantity royal icing (see page 106)

Equipment

Rolling pin

Small sharp knife

Carving knife

30cm (12in) round cake board

Cake smoothers (optional)

Palette knife (metal spatula)

Fine and medium paintbrushes

Sieve

About 30cm (12in) thread

1 First make the gelatine or modelling paste components as these will need time to dry. Make at least two (in case of breakages!) strips for the bridge. They should be about 7 x 4cm (6½ x 1½in) long and 5mm (¼in) thick. You can knead a little brown food colour into the paste before rolling it out or leave it white and paint later when in position.

2 Make two or three figures in case of mistakes (see page 110). Ensure that their bases are flat so that they can stand. Leave the figures and bridge to harden overnight, turning at least once.

3 Cut the cake in half diagonally. The cut should be slightly wavy to give the cliffs a more natural feel. Stand the pieces on their sides so they now form two triangular shapes. If you wish, you can split them and fill with a couple of layers of buttercream. Reassemble and spread a covering of buttercream all over.

4 To make the marbled rock-effect sugarpaste (rolled fondant), pull the grey sugarpaste into pieces and partially knead and roll it into the white (see Fishing cake on page 82). Use half of the sugarpaste to cover each rock. If it gathers into folds at the back, this does not matter, as the more irregular the sugarpaste, the more natural the rock will look. Simply scrunch up and cut away any surplus, trim and neaten. Roll any leftovers into rounded shapes for rocks.

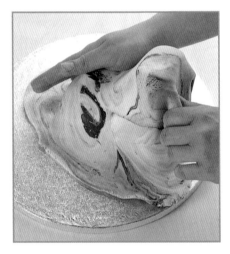

5 Place the cakes into position on the board. Partially mix a little blue food colour into about 4 heaped tablespoons of royal icing and swirl around the board, preferably using a palette knife (metal spatula) (see Fishing cake on page 82). Place the extra rocks into the water around the base of the cakes.

6 Balance the bridge across the ravine and glue in place with a little royal icing. If the bridge is too long, score a line across the strip and carefully snap off the excess. Lightly paint the bridge with a little brown food colour. Try not to soak the bridge

– if it gets too wet it will bend. Paint a few black lines to look like boards. Alternatively, to avoid potential damage when painting the bridge, you could just leave it white.

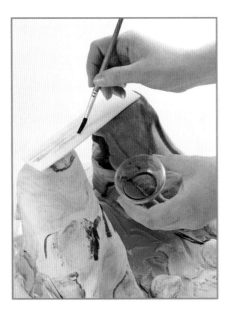

7 Lightly paint a figure with a little food colour trying to make it look a little like the recipient. Leave to dry.

8 To make the bushes, push pieces of both shades of green sugarpaste through a sieve (see Golf cake on page 48) and stick to the sides of the cliffs with a

QUICK & EASY VERSION

Here we have a wedding cake pillar masquerading as an ancient Greek monument from which the jumper has just unsuccessfully leapt! Daub some watery green food colour or edible dusting powder around the top of the cake. Make a couple of sugarpaste boots and stick them upside down on the cake. Stand the pillar behind the boots. Pipe a little green royal icing or buttercream grass around the base. Wrap and tie a length of thread around the boots a couple of times and rest the end on top of the pillar. Keep it in place with a disc of white sugarpaste, stuck to the pillar with a little water. Paint a few black food colour cracks around the boots and pipe extra grass/ivy up and over the pillar. If you wish, finish off with some simple flowers.

little water. Make more undergrowth and use it to camouflage the edges of the bridge.

9 When both the jumper and bridge are dry, tie one end of the thread around the jumper's feet and the other around the bridge. Stand the jumper on the edge. Get everyone to sing 'Happy Birthday', blow out the candles and push him off!

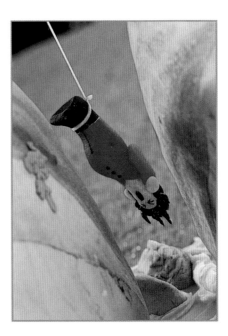

TROPHY

This versatile cake would be ideal for any sport. Feel free to alter the colours to suit your favourite team. If you want to save time, you could leave the board un-iced or omit the spots if piping makes you dotty!

1 Cover the cake board using the all-in-one method (see page 109). Moisten the entire board with a little water. Dust a work surface with icing (confectioners') sugar and knead 300g (10oz) white sugarpaste (rolled fondant) until pliable. Begin to roll, then transfer on to the damp cake board. Continue to roll the sugarpaste up to and over the edges. Neaten the edges and place to one side.

2 Level the top of the pudding bowl and slice the entire cake into two pieces. The section that will form the top of the cup should be slightly bigger than the base.

3 Lie both sections of the cake down so that the cut sides are flat on the work surface and slice both sections in half horizontally. Fill with buttercream and reassemble. Coat the outsides of both cakes with buttercream.

4 To cover the top of the cup, roll out all of the grey sugarpaste quite thickly (about

1cm/⅓in) and place over the top of the cake. Trim and neaten the base. Keep the excess for making the handles later.

5 Cover the base of the cup with the black sugarpaste. Smooth it into position and again trim and neaten the base. Carefully lift and place both cakes on to the covered cake board.

6 Roll about 30g (1oz) of the leftover grey sugarpaste into a thick disc shape for the stem. Stick it in place between the two cakes.

7 For the trophy handles, make two 30g (1oz) sausage shapes from the leftover grey sugarpaste and stick next to the top cake in an S shape.

TIP
You could use a fish slice to lift the cakes to avoid getting fingerprints in the icing.

Cake and Decoration

1 sponge (layer) cake baked in a pudding bowl (see page 105)
½ quantity buttercream (see page 106)
Icing (confectioners') sugar for rolling out
Water for sticking sugarpaste (rolled fondant)
350g (12oz) white sugarpaste
400g (13oz) grey sugarpaste
250g (8oz) black sugarpaste
120g (4oz) red sugarpaste
60g (2oz) blue sugarpaste
Black and blue food colour pastes
1 tablespoon royal icing (optional) (see page 106)

Equipment

30cm (12in) round cake board
Rolling pin
Small sharp knife
Carving knife
Cake smoothers (optional)
Garrett frill cutter (optional)
Cocktail stick (toothpick)
Paintbrushes (fine and medium)
No. 2 piping tube (tip) (optional)
Piping bag (optional) (see page 107)
Scissors

8 To make the rosette, begin with the ribbon tails. Roll out 60g (2oz) red sugarpaste and cut out two strips. Cut a point in the end of each and stick in place.

9 To make the head of the rosette, ideally you need a frill cutter, but all is not lost if you do not have one. If you do have one, roll out about 45g (1½oz) blue sugarpaste and cut out a frilly circle. Slide a knife under the sugarpaste to loosen it. Dust your work surface with icing sugar to prevent sticking, and roll a cocktail stick (toothpick) around the edge of the circle. Like magic you should see a frill starting to develop. Do not worry about icing sugar marks, they will be dealt with at the end.

10 Either stick the frilly circle as it is on to the side of the cake or if you want a larger rosette cut the frill and stick in a larger circle. Then roll out some more blue and frill, as before. Use as much as necessary of this second frill to make up the shortfall on the first.

11 If you do not have a frill cutter, roll out the blue sugarpaste and cut out a disc with a wavy edge. It doesn't have to be 100 per cent accurate. Cut a hole out of the centre and follow the rest of steps 9 and 10 until you have created the base of the rosette.

12 Continue to build up the rosette with alternating colours, then stick a flat disc of white in the centre. Paint a number 1 with black food colour.

13 Place a no. 2 piping tube (tip) into a piping bag. Colour about 1 tablespoon of royal icing or buttercream blue and pipe dots around the board.

14 Using a soft, damp paintbrush, wipe away any icing sugar marks around the frill and the rest of the cake. The icing will look shiny temporarily but this will dry to a matt finish after a few hours.

QUICK & EASY VERSIONS

For the medal cake, drape the first ribbon behind the medal in a V shape and fasten the ends with royal icing or buttercream. Wrap a second length of ribbon around the cake and secure at the back. A large chocolate coin makes an ideal medal, or paint a sugarpaste disc with edible gold food colour.

On the cup cake, the bowl of the cup is made from a grey sugarpaste disc with a section sliced off the top. Repeat with a smaller black sugarpaste disc for the base, Add a grey sugarpaste rectangle for the stem and bend and stick two grey sugarpaste sausages into S shapes for the handles. Finish off with a bow, stuck to the cup with buttercream or royal icing.

BAKING RECIPES

EASY MADEIRA SPONGE (LAYER) CAKE

Many people think that baking a cake is much more complicated than it actually is. Just to prove it, here is an extremely easy recipe. You just throw everything into a bowl, mix and bake. It tastes delicious, and can be frozen for up to three months.

Square tin (pan)		15cm (6in)	18cm (7in)	20cm (8in)	25cm (10in)
Round tin (pan)	15cm (6in)	18cm (7in)	20cm (8in)	23cm (9in)	
Self-raising flour	175g (6oz/1½ cups)	225g (8oz/2 cups)	290g (10oz/2½ cups)	350g (12oz/3 cups)	500g (1lb 2oz/4½ cups)
Caster (superfine) sugar	120g (4oz/½ cup)	175g (6oz/¾ cup)	225g (8oz/1 cup)	290g (10oz/1¼cups)	450g (1lb/2 cups)
Butter (soft)	120g (4oz/½ cup)	175g (6oz/¾ cup)	225g (8oz/1 cup)	290g (10oz/1¼cups)	450g (1lb/2 cups)
Eggs (medium)	2	3	4	5	9
Milk	15ml (1 tbsp)	30ml (2 tbsp)	30ml (2 tbsp)	45ml (3 tbsp)	60ml (4 tbsp)
Baking time (approx)	1¼hrs	1¼ hrs	1¾ hrs	2 hrs	2¼ hrs

1 Grease and line the tin (pan). Preheat the oven to 150°C/300°F/Gas mark 2.
2 Sift the flour into a mixing bowl and add the rest of the ingredients. Start the mixer on a slow speed to bind together the ingredients, then increase and beat on a faster speed for 1 minute until the mixture is pale and smooth.

3 Spoon into the prepared tin and bake in the centre of the oven.
4 To test whether it is ready, listen to it! If there are still a lot of bubbling sounds, it is probably not ready. Give it a further 10 minutes. Test by inserting a knife or skewer. If it comes out clean, the cake is done. Leave in the tin for 5 minutes,

then turn out on to a wire rack. Peel away the lining paper and leave to cool.

NOTES: The top of the cake may rise and crack. This is not a disaster as the crust is usually cut off before the cake is decorated. For fan ovens, decrease the temperature by 20°C.

CHOCOLATE CAKE

This is a luscious chocolate cake with an almost velvety texture. While it is cooking, a crust will form on top. It may even scorch slightly. This is nothing to worry about, as the crust will be cut off before decorating. It is not absolutely essential, but for the best taste use chocolate with a high percentage of cocoa solids (about 70 per cent). The cake can be frozen for up to three months.

Square tin (pan)		15cm (6in)	18cm (7in)	20cm (8in)	25cm (10in)
Round tin (pan)	15cm (6in)	18cm (7in)	20cm (8in)	23cm (9in)	
Eggs (medium, separated)	3	4	6	8	10
Plain (dark) chocolate	150g (5oz)	175g (6oz)	225g (8oz)	290g (10oz)	425g (14oz)
Butter	90g (3oz/⅓ cup)	120g (4oz/½ cup)	175g (6oz/¾ cup)	225g (8oz/1 cup)	290g (10oz/1¼ cups)
Caster (superfine) sugar	45g (1½oz/3 tbsp)	75g (2¼oz/5 tbsp)	120g (4oz/½ cup)	175g (6oz/¾ cup)	200g (6½oz/generous ¾ cup)
Self-raising flour	90g (3oz/¾ cup)	120g (4oz/1 cup)	175g (6oz/1½ cups)	225g (8oz/2 cups)	290g (10oz/2½ cups)
Icing (confectioners') sugar	30g (1oz/¼ cup)	30g (1oz/¼ cup)	60g (2oz/½ cup)	75g (2½oz/⅔ cup)	90g (3oz/¾ cup)
Baking times (approx)	45 mins	1 hr	1¼ hrs	1¼ hrs	1½ hrs

1 Preheat the oven to 180°C/350°F/Gas mark 4. Grease and line the relevant cake tin (pan). Separate the eggs.
2 Melt the chocolate. Cream the butter and sugar together in a mixing bowl, beat in the egg yolks and then the chocolate.
3 Set the mixer to a slow speed and fold in the sifted flour.
4 Scrape the chocolate mixture into

a spare bowl. Wash and dry the mixing bowl, making sure it is grease-free.
5 Place the egg whites in the clean bowl and whisk into stiff peaks. Whisk in the sifted icing (confectioners') sugar.
6 Slowly mix the chocolate mixture into the egg whites. Pour into the tin. Bake immediately.
7 Because a crust forms on top, you

cannot tell by touch alone if it is cooked. There should be a strong smell of chocolate, and you should not be able to hear any bubbling from inside the cake. To be doubly sure, cut away a little crust from the centre, and insert a skewer or knife. If it comes out clean, the cake is ready. If not, replace the cut crust and cook a further 10 minutes.

FRUIT CAKE

There is no mystery to baking a good fruit cake. Purists advise that you make your fruit cake three months in advance of the date it is required, and then feed it weekly with alcohol. If you have time, great; if not, do not despair. This recipe produces a cake that will be delicious after three months, a week or even as soon as it has cooled down!

Square tin (pan)	15cm (6in)	18cm (7in)	20cm (8in)	25cm (10in)
Round tin (pan)	18cm (7in)	20cm (8in)	23cm (9in)	
Currants	150g (5oz/1 cup)	175g (6oz/1 cup)	200g (7oz/1¼ cups)	450g (1lb/2½ cups)
Sultanas (golden raisins)	150g (5oz/1 cup)	175g (6oz/1 cup)	200g (7oz/1¼ cups)	450g (1lb/2½ cups)
Raisins	150g (5oz/1 cup)	175g (6oz/1 cup)	200g (7oz/1¼ cups)	450g (1lb/2½ cups)
Mixed peel	30g (1oz/¼ cup)	45g (1½oz/⅓ cup)	60g (2oz/½ cup)	120g (4oz/1 cup)
Glacé (candied) cherries (halved)	60g (2oz/½ cup)	75g (2½oz/⅔ cup)	90g (3oz/¾ cup)	150g (5oz/1¼ cups)
Brandy	60ml (4 tbsp)	75ml (5 tbsp)	90ml (6 tbsp)	105ml (7 tbsp)
Butter	150g (5oz/⅔ cup)	175g (6oz/¾ cup)	200g (7oz/⅞ cup)	450g (1lb/2 cups)
Dark brown sugar	150g (5oz/¾ cup)	175g (6oz/1 cup)	200g (7oz/1¼ cups)	450g (1lb/2½ cups)
Eggs (medium)	3	4	6	10
Plain (all-purpose) flour	175g (6oz/1½ cups)	210g (7oz/1¾ cups)	250g (9oz/2¼ cups)	500g (1lb 2oz/4½ cups)
Mixed spice	1 tsp	1 tsp	1½ tsp	1 tbsp
Cinnamon	1 tsp	1 tsp	1½ tsp	1 tbsp
Ground almonds	30g (1oz/¼ cup)	45g (1½oz/⅓ cup)	60g (2oz/½ cup)	120g (4oz/1 cup)
Lemon (zest only)	1	1	1	2
Flaked almonds	30g (1oz/¼ cup)	45g (1½oz/⅓ cup)	60g (2oz/½ cup)	120g (4oz/1 cup)
Baking time (approx)	2–2¼ hrs	2¼–2½ hrs	2½–3 hrs	3–3¼ hrs

1 Place the dried fruits in a mixing bowl. Pour over the brandy and stir. Cover and leave for about 6 hours or, preferably, overnight.
2 Grease and double line the relevant cake tin (pan) with greaseproof paper (baking parchment). Wrap a double layer of greaseproof around the outside of the tin and tie string around to secure.
3 Preheat the oven to 150°C/300°F/Gas mark 2.
4 Cream together the butter and dark brown sugar, then beat in the eggs. Gently stir in the sifted flour, spices and ground almonds. Add a little more flour if the mixture looks runny.
5 Stir in the soaked fruits, grated lemon zest and flaked almonds.
6 Spoon into the tin. Bake for the required time. Insert a skewer or clean, sharp knife into the centre. If it comes out clean, the cake is ready. Otherwise, bake for a further 15 minutes and test again. Leave the cake to cool in the tin.

STORING A FRUIT CAKE
To keep a fruit cake for up to three months, pierce the top with a cocktail stick (toothpick) several times and drizzle with a little brandy. Double-wrap the cake in greaseproof and two sheets of foil. Keep in a tin or cupboard, but not an airtight plastic container. Drizzle with extra brandy every week or so.

WORKING WITH FRUIT CAKE
You cannot place sugarpaste (rolled fondant) directly on to fruit cake. Instead, carve the cake into the required shape and drizzle with a little brandy if you wish. Brush the sides with boiled apricot jam and roll out some marzipan on a surface dusted with icing (confectioners') sugar. Cover the cake, smoothing the marzipan into position. Trim and neaten the base. Moisten the marzipan with a little cooled, boiled water and cover with the sugarpaste. Smooth and neaten as usual.

MAKING TRUFFLES
When carving a cake into an unusual shape, you often find you have pieces left over. It is easy to make little cake truffles using vanilla, chocolate or fruit cake and any type of chocolate (milk, plain or white). You need about 30g (1oz) of chocolate to every 30g (1oz) of cake crumbs. Use any combination of cake and chocolate (Madeira and white chocolate go particularly well). Simply melt the chocolate, stir in the cake crumbs and roll into little balls.

BAKING CAKES IN PUDDING BOWLS OR LOAF TINS (PANS)
If you use a 1 litre (1¾ pint/4¼ cup) heatproof pudding bowl or 1kg (2lb) loaf tin (pan) for cakes such as Trophy or Aerobics, they will be shaped ready for decorating, with no waste. Use quantities given for a 15cm (6in) square cake.
Grease the inside of the bowl and place a disc of greaseproof paper in the base. Do the same with the loaf tin, using a strip of greaseproof paper instead. When the cake is cooked, slide a knife around the edges to loosen it. Turn out to cool.

ICING RECIPES

SUGARPASTE (ROLLED FONDANT)

You should be able to buy sugarpaste (rolled fondant) ready-made at the supermarket or any cake-decorating supplier. It might be called something like 'ready to roll', 'fondant' or 'easy modelling' icing. Alternatively, you can make your own.

ingredients

500g (1lb 2oz/4½cups) icing (confectioners') sugar

1 egg white (or the equivalent amount of dried egg white mixed with the amount of water recommended on the packet)

30ml (2 tablespoons) liquid glucose (see gelatine icing introduction, page 107)

1 Place the icing (confectioners') sugar into a large mixing bowl.
2 Make a well in the centre and add the egg white and liquid glucose.
3 Begin to bind together the mixture with a wooden spoon, then use your hands and knead until all the sugar is mixed in and the icing is smooth.
4 Sugarpaste can be used straight away. Store in a plastic bag until required.

COLOURING SUGARPASTE

Sugarpaste can be bought ready-coloured, but you can create your own colours by adding food-colouring *pastes* in different combinations and proportions. These can be bought from supermarkets and specialist cake decorating shops. The more you knead in, the deeper the colour. You can use disposable plastic gloves from the supermarket to protect your hands if you wish.

• To make flesh-coloured sugarpaste for white characters, use paprika food-colour paste or knead a little pink and yellow sugarpaste into white. For darker skin tones, use chestnut or brown food-colour pastes.
• To make purple, use grape violet food-colour paste (or use a ready-coloured sugarpaste shade called Blackcurrant).
• To make turquoise, knead green and blue food-colour paste into sugarpaste.

BUTTERCREAM

ingredients (1 quantity)

250g (8oz/1 cup) softened butter

450g (1lb/4 cups) sifted icing (confectioners') sugar

1 teaspoon vanilla essence (extract)

1 tablespoon hot water

Beat the butter until soft and fluffy then add the rest of the ingredients. Beat until it can be easily spread.

FLAVOUR VARIATIONS

Chocolate: mix 100g (3½oz) melted plain or white chocolate into the buttercream. Or mix 1 tablespoon cocoa powder and 1–2 tablespoons hot water into a paste and add.
Coffee: Mix 1 tablespoon instant coffee into 1 tablespoon hot water and beat into the buttercream.
Alternative flavourings: Instead of vanilla essence you could use peppermint, almond or lemon.

ROYAL ICING

Traditionally, royal icing is made with real egg white, but dried egg white works just as well. It also cuts out the small risk of salmonella poisoning. Always read the instructions in case they are different from those given here. For our purposes, food-colour paste is perfect for colouring royal icing.

ingredients (with dried egg white)

1 tablespoon/20g (½oz) dried egg white

500g (1lb 2oz/4½ cups) icing (confectioners') sugar

90ml (2½fl oz/5 tablespoons) cold water

1 Stir the egg white into the sifted icing (confectioners') sugar.
2 Add the water and beat on a slow speed for about 5 minutes until the icing stands in peaks.
3 Put the icing in an airtight plastic container with a lid. Place plastic wrap on top of the icing and close with the lid. Keep it covered when not in use.
4 When required, take out the amount of royal icing needed and re-seal the container. Stir the icing briskly to expel air bubbles.

ingredients (with fresh egg white)

2 egg whites

¼ teaspoon lemon juice

500g (1lb 2oz/4½ cups) icing (confectioners') sugar

5ml (1 teaspoon) glycerine

1 Place the egg whites into a grease-free bowl and add the lemon juice.
2 Sift in a little icing (confectioners') sugar and stir. Add more and stir again.
3 Beat until the icing has reached the desired consistency. Store as for the royal icing made with dried egg whites.

GELATINE AND MODELLING ICING

These icings have much the same properties. They will both set hard and are perfect for moulded shapes that you want to stand up. The modelling icing is suitable for vegetarians, as the vegetarian equivalent of gelatine does not work. Use whichever type suits you best. Gum tragacanth and liquid glucose are available from cake-decorating shops. You should also be able to find liquid glucose at the supermarket or a chemist.

gelatine icing ingredients

60ml (4 tablespoons) cold water

1 sachet (about 12g/½oz) gelatine powder (enough to set 600ml/1 pint/2½ cups)

10ml (2 teaspoons) liquid glucose

500g (1lb 2oz/4½cups) icing (confectioners') sugar

Cornflour (cornstarch) as required

1 Place the water in a small heatproof bowl and sprinkle the gelatine over the top. Leave for about 2 minutes until it has soaked up all the water.
2 Stand the bowl in about 1cm (½in) water in a saucepan and heat gently until dissolved.

3 Remove the bowl from the water and stir in the liquid glucose.
4 Sift the icing (confectioners') sugar into a mixing bowl and make a well in the centre.
5 Add the glucose mixture and stir in with a knife.
6 Knead into a dough-like consistency adding cornflour (cornstarch) if required. Double-wrap in two plastic bags until required.
7 Gelatine icing can be used straight away and does not need to be stored in the refrigerator. If it has hardened slightly, microwave on full power for 3–5 seconds to soften. Colour can be either kneaded in at this stage or painted on after the icing has dried.

modelling icing ingredients

500g (1lb 2oz/4½ cups) icing (confectioners') sugar

30ml (2 tablespoons) gum tragacanth

10ml (2 teaspoons) liquid glucose

60ml (4 tablespoons) cold water

Cornflour (cornstarch) as required

1 Mix the icing (confectioners') sugar and gum tragacanth in a bowl and make a well in the centre.
2 Pour in the glucose and water, then mix. Dust a work surface with cornflour and knead the icing to a dough-like consistency. Double-wrap in two plastic bags and leave for about 8 hours.

MAKING A PIPING BAG

You can buy ready-made disposable or re-usable piping bags from cake decorating equipment shops, but it is not that difficult to make your own.

1 Fold a 30cm (12in) square of greaseproof paper (baking parchment) in half diagonally and slide a knife along the crease to cut it. One triangle will make one bag.

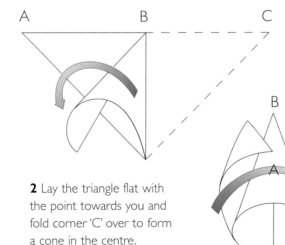

2 Lay the triangle flat with the point towards you and fold corner 'C' over to form a cone in the centre.

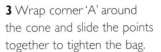

3 Wrap corner 'A' around the cone and slide the points together to tighten the bag.

4 Fold the top point over twice to hold it together. If using a piping tube (tip), snip a triangle off the end. Insert the tube and icing and fold over the top of the bag twice to close. If you are not using a tube, place the icing inside, fold the end to close and then snip a tiny triangle off the end.

TECHNIQUES

Here are some hints and tips on how to achieve special effects, get out of trouble and generally perfect your sporty cake creations.

WORKING WITH SUGARPASTE (ROLLED FONDANT)

• Always knead and roll out sugarpaste on icing (confectioners') sugar, never flour. In fact, always keep a bowl of icing sugar handy to stop your fingers from getting sticky.

• To get rid of any icing sugar smudges when you have finished your cake, lightly brush them away with a soft, damp paintbrush. Initially, the sugarpaste will look shiny but it will dry to a matt finish after a couple of hours.

• All these cakes are designed so that you need use only cooled boiled water for sticking your models together.

COLOURING SUGARPASTE

You can buy some sugarpaste ready coloured, but if colouring your own, always use paste colours or gels. Liquid colours make the icing soggy. If this happens, try kneading in a little icing (confectioners') sugar. Apply the colour with a clean knife or a cocktail stick (toothpick). Knead in until you have a good flat colour. You can also knead together two colours of sugarpaste to obtain a different shade (see page 106).

WOODGRAIN EFFECT

This looks realistic and is easy to do. Roll together some brown and white sugarpaste to form a sausage shape. Fold in half, re-roll and fold in half again. Repeat 8–10 times, until a woodgrain effect appears. Roll out. Use as normal.

MARBLING

You can see this effect on the Water-skiing and Swimming cakes (see pages 10 and 22). Again, it is very easy to create. Apply a little food colour paste to the sugarpaste and slowly begin to knead it in. Stop before the sugarpaste becomes one solid colour, then roll out and use as normal.

ROCKS

Stick a few lumps of black or grey on to some white sugarpaste, and partially knead together the two colours. Stop before it becomes a solid colour. Pull off little pieces and roll into small or large pebble shapes.

FRILLING AND PLEATING

These are two effective and easy-to-do little tricks. To obtain a pleated effect, which is great for items such as netball skirts, simply cut out the shape and press a paintbrush handle along the sugarpaste to leave a groove. Continue all the way along the strip.

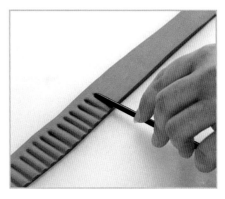

To frill, roll a cocktail stick (toothpick) or end of paintbrush along the edge of some rolled-out sugarpaste in a backward and forward motion.

PAINTING ON SUGARPASTE

Painting on sugarpaste is not as daunting as it might seem because you can always get rid of mistakes. Use watered-down food-colour pastes, with a saucer as a palette. Use different paint brushes from any you might use with conventional paint, and store separately.

Treat the medium as you would watercolour. If you want your image to have an outline, paint it in after you have coloured the middle, or the black food paste will bleed into the colour. If you make a mistake, dab it with a clean brush dipped in clean water to break it down. Then wipe away with a clean, damp cloth.

COVERING CAKES

Knead the sugarpaste (rolled fondant) until warm and pliable. Roll out on icing (confectioners') sugar to a thickness of 5mm (1/4in). As a rough guide, you need to roll it out to about 15cm (6in) wider than the top of your cake to allow enough icing for the sides. Lift and place over the cake. Starting from the top to prevent air bubbles forming, smooth the icing into place, then work down over the sides. A cake smoother is a great help when doing this. You simply use it to iron out lumps and bumps.

THE DREADED AIR BUBBLE

If you find a bubble has formed under the icing and you cannot ease it out, prick it with a clean dressmaker's pin held at an angle and press out the air.

COVERING CAKE BOARDS
ALL-IN-ONE

This is the easiest way to cover a cake board and it is best done before the cake is positioned on top. Moisten the cake board with water and begin to roll out the sugarpaste. Lift and place the piece of sugarpaste directly on to the board and continue to roll it up to and over the edges. Run a sharp knife around the edge of the board to neaten it. The only drawback to this method of covering the board is that the icing beneath the cake will eventually start to go soggy. But you will probably find that your delicious cake has disappeared long before that becomes a real problem!

FOUR STRIPS

This is a simple way to cover a square cake board around an already covered square cake. Moisten the exposed cake board with a little water. Roll out a piece of sugarpaste, cut four strips and lay one along each edge of the board. Using a sharp knife, make a diagonal cut from each corner of the board towards the corner of the cake. Peel away the excess. Trim away any overhang along the edges of the board.

BANDAGE METHOD

This is the easiest way to cover the board around a round, covered cake. Moisten the board. Measure the circumference of the cake and roll out a strip of sugarpaste to that length. Cut a little paste off one of the long edges to neaten. Roll up the sugarpaste like a loose bandage. Starting from the back, unwind it around the board. Smooth it into position and neaten the edges.

COLOURING DESICCATED (SHREDDED) COCONUT

Place the required amount of coconut in a small bowl and add food-colour paste. Mix it in with your hand, wearing a disposable glove to prevent staining.

TEMPLATES

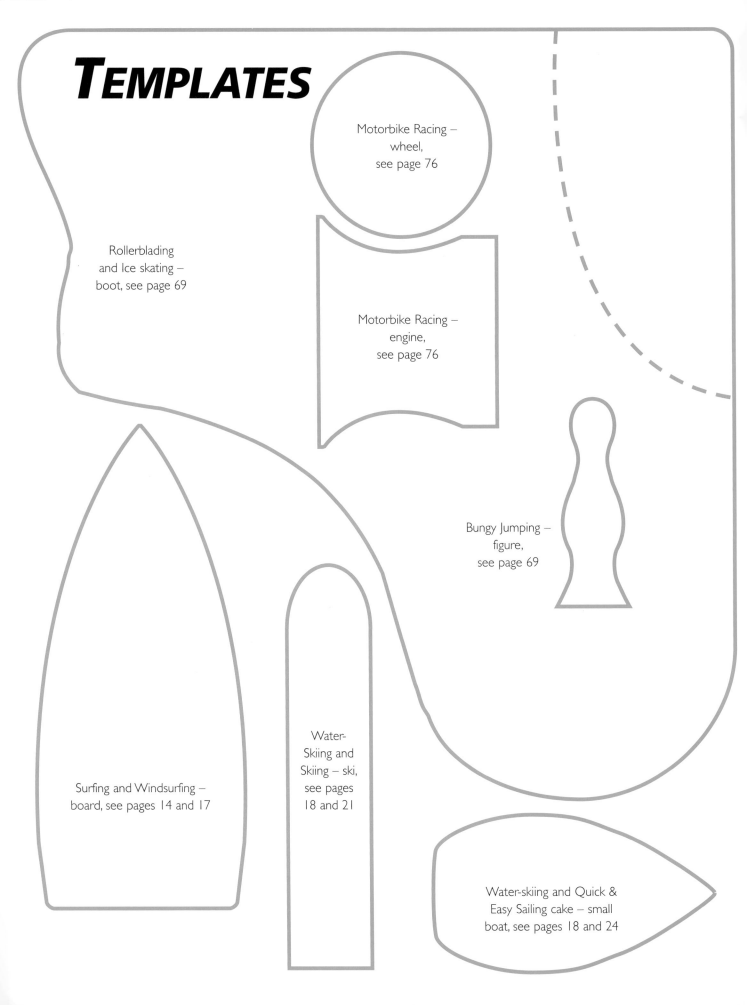

Motorbike Racing –
wheel,
see page 76

Rollerblading
and Ice skating –
boot, see page 69

Motorbike Racing –
engine,
see page 76

Bungy Jumping –
figure,
see page 69

Surfing and Windsurfing –
board, see pages 14 and 17

Water-
Skiing and
Skiing – ski,
see pages
18 and 21

Water-skiing and Quick &
Easy Sailing cake – small
boat, see pages 18 and 24

INDEX

First published in 2000 by **Merehurst Limited**, Ferry House, 51–57 Lacy Road, Putney, London SW15 1PR

Copyright © Carol Deacon 2000 Photography © Merehurst Limited

Carol Deacon has asserted her rights under the Copyright, Designs and Patents Act, 1988

ISBN 1 85391 945 4

Commissioning Editor: **Barbara Croxford**

Art Direction: **Helen Taylor**

Design: **Studio Cactus**

Jacket Design: **Anita Ruddell**

Photographer: **Edward Allwright**

Photographer's Assistant: **John Stokes**

Production Manager: **Lucy Byrne**

Publishing Manager: **Fia Fornari**

Publisher: **Catie Ziller**

Marketing & Sales Director: **Kathryn Harvey**

International Sales Director: **Kevin Lagden**

CEO: **Robert Oerton**

Colour separation by Colour Connection UK

Printed in Dubai by Oriental Press

Contact Carol Deacon at:
E-MAIL caroldeacon@hotmail.com
WEBSITE www.caroldeacon.com

SPECIALIST STOCKISTS

Here is a selection of cake-decorating equipment shops and retail outlets. Most of them offer a mail-order service. Alternatively, look up your nearest shop in the phone book, or call Culpitt's Customer Service line on 01670 842800 to find out which is the closest.

THE CAKE MAKER'S DEPOT
57 The Tything, Worcester
WR1 1TJ, UK
Tel: 01905 25468

CAKES & CO.
25 Rock Hill, Blackrock Village,
Co. Dublin, Ireland
Tel: + 353 1 282 6544

CONFECTIONERY SUPPLIES
29–31 Lower Cathedral Road,
Cardiff, CF1 8LU, UK
Tel: 029 2037 2161
Fax: 029 2039 6632
(Also in Bristol, Hereford and Swansea)

CORTEIL & BARRATT
40 High Street, Ewell Village, Epsom,
Surrey, KT17 1RW, UK
Tel: 020 8393 0032
Fax: 020 8786 8779

CREATIVE CAKES & SUPPLIES
379 Clarkston Road, Cathcart, Glasgow,
G44 3JG, UK
Tel: 0141 633 0392

CULPITT LTD
Jubilee Industrial Estate,
Ashington, Northumberland,
NE63 8UQ, UK
Customer service line: 01670 842800
Tel: 01670 814545
Fax: 0800 801235
Website: www.culpitt.com

GUY, PAUL & CO. LTD
Unit B4, Foundry Way,
Little End Road, Eaton Socon,
Cambs PE19 3JH, UK
Tel: 01480 472545
Fax: 01480 405608

LINDEN CAKE GALLERY
15 Cross Street, Wakefield,
WF1 3BW, UK
Tel: 01924 299449

LONDON SUGARART CENTRE
12 Selkirk Road, London SW17, UK
Tel: 020 8767 8558
Fax: 020 8767 9939

PIPEDREAMS
2 Bell Lane, Eton Wick, Berkshire, UK
Tel: 01753 865682

RENSHAW SCOTT LTD
Crown Street, Liverpool, L8 7RF, UK
Tel: 0151 706 8282
Fax: 0151 706 8201
Clyde Street, Carluke, ML8 5BD, UK
Tel: 01555 770711
www.renshawscott.co.uk

SQUIRES KITCHEN
Squires House, 3 Waverley Lane,
Farnham, Surrey, GU9 8BB, UK
Tel: + 44 1252 711 749

TORBAY CAKE CRAFT
5 Seaway Road, Preston, Paignton,
Devon, TQ3 2NX, UK
Tel & Fax: 01803 550178

Australia/New Zealand
CAKE AND ICING CENTRE
651 Samford Road, Mitchelton,
Queensland 4053, Australia
Tel: + 61 7 3355 3443

CAKE DECORATORS' SUPPLIES
Shop 1, 770 George Street,
Sydney 2001, Australia
Tel: + 61 2 9212 4050

THE CAKE DECORATING CENTRE
1 Adelaide Arcade, Adelaide
South Australia 5000
Tel: + 61 8 8223 1719

FINISHING TOUCHES CAKE DECORATING CENTRE
268 Centre Road, Bentleigh
Victoria 3204, Australia
Tel: + 61 3 9223 1719

STARLINE DISTRIBUTORS LTD
28 Jessie Street, Wellington, New Zealand
Tel: + 64 4 383 7424

USA
BERYL'S CAKE DECORATING & PASTRY SUPPLIES
P.O. Box 1584, N. Springfield, VA22151-0584, USA
Tel: + 1 800 488 2749
Fax: + 1 703 750 3779

ACKNOWLEDGEMENTS

The author and publisher would like to thank Renshaw Scott Ltd for supplying Regalice sugarpaste; Guy, Paul & Co. Ltd for cake boards; and Culpitt Ltd for equipment.

Carol Deacon would also personally like to thank photographer Edward Allwright and his assistant, John Stokes, for the magnificent sausage and egg sandwiches they provided on the shoot. Oh, and their work wasn't all that bad either!

Carol would also like to thank her husband, Chris, for putting up with a house full of cake boxes, and for sorting out a computer virus that nearly wiped the entire book off her computer.

Finally, Carol would like to apologise to Merehurst Ltd for infecting them with the aforementioned virus and hopes this does not mean they will never work with her again!